暖小昕 / 编译

My World Is
Very Small,
But Just Sweet

我的世界很小，
但是刚刚好

每天读一点暖心英文

北京联合出版公司
Beijing United Publishing Co.,Ltd.

图书在版编目（CIP）数据

我的世界很小，但是刚刚好 ：汉英对照 / 暖小昕编
译. — 北京 ：北京联合出版公司，2015.4（2015.6重印）
（每天读一点暖心英文）
ISBN 978-7-5502-4903-5

Ⅰ. ①我… Ⅱ. ①暖… Ⅲ. ①英语－汉语－对照读物
②散文集－世界 Ⅳ. ①H319.4：I

中国版本图书馆CIP数据核字(2015)第055045号

我的世界很小，但是刚刚好

编　　译：暖小昕
选题策划：范彦凤
责任编辑：丰雪飞
封面设计：马顾本
版式设计：王国蕊
责任校对：王抗抗

北京联合出版公司出版
（北京市西城区德外大街83号楼9层　100088）
小森（北京）印刷有限公司　新华书店经销
字数100千字　787毫米×1208毫米　1/32　6印张
2015年5月第1版　2015年6月第2次印刷
ISBN 978-7-5502-4903-5
定价：25.00元

目　录
CONTENTS

逝去的爱
First Love

[美] 约翰·沃尔特斯 / John Walters

我记得，当时的阳光洒落在她的发丝上。她转过头，我们四目相对，在那间吵闹的五年级教室里，我感觉到了一些东西，觉得心底遭到了一击。我的初恋就此开始了。

她叫雷切尔，我从小学到中学一直很迷恋她，看到她，我的心就怦怦地跳，有她在时，我说话就有些结巴。我就像夏日里一只不幸的小昆虫，被一扇窗前微弱的灯光吸引，在黑暗的夜晚徘徊在她的窗前。

当看到她上学或是放学回家，走在林荫小路上时，我整个人就呆住了，她看起来总是那么镇定自若。在家时，我回想着与她的每一次邂逅，一想到自己的不足之处便心生懊恼。即便如此，当我们正值青春年少时，我仍然感受到她对我深情的宽容。

我们还不够成熟，根本不可能发展稳定的恋爱关系。她自幼受正统犹太教的家庭熏陶，而我因信奉天主教心存顾忌，这使我们表现得清心寡欲，有如谦谦君子，就连亲吻都遥不可及，无论这种渴望是多么强烈。在一场舞会上，我设法拥抱了她一下——当然，有大人在场。我们的拥抱让她咯咯地笑了起来，她那纯洁干脆的笑声让我痛恨自己所想的一切。

总而言之，我对雷切尔的爱一直是单恋。中学毕业后，她考上了大学，我参了军。第二次世界大战爆发后，我被派到海外。有一段时间，我们保持着联系，她的来信成为那些难熬的漫长岁月中的一抹亮色。有一次，她给我寄了一张她的泳装照，我浮想联翩，在回信里提到是否可能结婚。她的回信几乎立即少了，也很少提及个人的事情。

我回国后做的第一件事就是去找雷切尔。她母亲开了门，说雷切尔已经不住在这里了，她与在大学里认识的一个医学院的学生结了婚。"我还以为她写信通知你了。"她的母亲说。

我最终在等待复员时收到了她的"亲爱的约翰"一信。她委婉地解释了不能和我结婚的原因。回首过去，我真的恢复得很快，尽管在开始的几个月里，我认为自己活不下去了。就像雷切尔一样，我找到了另一个人，我学会用一种深情和永恒的责任感去爱她，而这种责任感一直延续到现在。

可是，最近，在相隔40余年之后，我接到了雷切尔打来的电话，她的丈夫过世了。她经过我所在的城镇，通过我们都认识的一个朋友打听到了我的住址，我们相约见面。

我感到好奇而兴奋，在过去的这些年里，我没有挂念过她，她突然在一个早晨给我打了电话，这让我很惊讶。见到她时，我又感到很震惊，这位坐在餐桌前，头发花白的女人就是我梦寐以求的雷切尔吗？就是那个照片上体态轻盈的美人鱼吗？

因为很久不见，我们互相寒暄，谈了共同关心的话题。我们就像老朋友那样聊天，很快发现我们都已经是祖父母了。

"你还记得这个吗？"她递给我一张破旧的纸条，那是我在学校时为她写的一首诗。我仔细看了这首格律粗糙、韵律苍白的诗。她望着我的脸，从我的手里把纸抢走，并装进了包里，好像很怕我会毁掉它。

我告诉她有关相片的事，告诉她我是如何带着它度过了整个战争。

"我们不可能在一起，这你是知道的。"她说。

"你为何如此确定？"我反问她，"哦，姑娘，我的爱尔兰道德感和你犹太人的责任心，那一定非常完美！"

我们的笑声惊动了旁边的人，在余下的时间里，我们都只是偷偷地看着对方。我想，我们从对方身上看到我们一直保留在心中的形象破灭了。

在我送她上出租车之前，她转向我，说："我只是想再看你一眼，告诉你一些事情。"她的双眼凝视着我，"我想谢谢你曾经那么爱我。"我们吻了一下，她离开了。

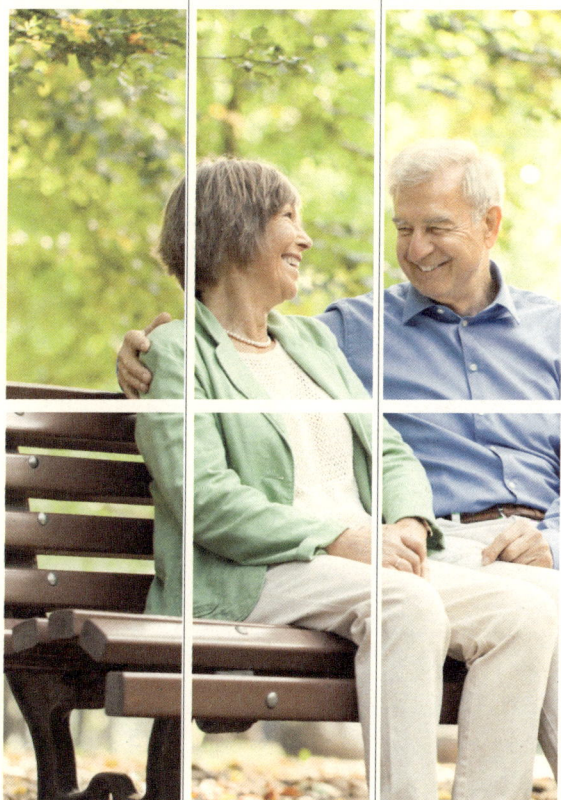

我在商店的橱窗里看见了自己：灰白的头发在晚风中拂动。我决定步行回家，她的吻还在我的唇上燃烧，我感到有点儿晕，于是坐在公园的一张长凳上。在我身旁，花草树木正在夕阳的照耀下熠熠发光，压在我心上的某个东西消失了，某件事情圆满了。我眼前的景象是如此之美，我快乐得想要叫喊，想要唱歌跳舞。

如同一切事物一样，这一切很快就过去了，不一会儿，我起身回家了。

I remember the way the light touched her hair. She turned her head, and our eyes met, a momentary awareness in that raucous fifth-grade classroom. I felt as though I'd been struck a blow under the heart. Thus began my first love affair.

Her name was Rachel, and I mooned my way through grade and high school, stricken at the mere sight of her, tongue-tied in her presence. Does anyone, anymore, linger in the shadows of evening, drawn by the pale light of a window—her window—like some hapless summer insect?

I would catch sight of her, walking down an aisle of trees to or from school, and I'd become paralyzed. She always seemed so poised, so self-possessed. At home, I'd relive each encounter, writhing at the thought of my inadequacies. Even so, as we entered our teens, I sensed her affectionate tolerance for me.

"Going steady" implied a maturity we still lacked. Her Orthodox Jewish upbringing and my own Catholic scruples imposed a celibate grace that made even kissing a distant prospect, however fervently desired. I managed to hold her once at a dance—chaperoned, of course. Our embrace made her giggle, a sound so trusting that I hated myself for what I'd been thinking.

At any rate, my love for Rachel remained unrequited. We graduated from high school, she went on to college, and I joined the Army. When World War II engulfed us, I was sent overseas. For a time we corresponded, and her letters were the highlight of those grinding, endless years. Once she sent me a snapshot of herself in a bathing suit, which drove me to the wildest of fantasies. I mentioned the possibility of marriage in my next letter, and almost immediately her replies became less frequent, less personal.

The first thing I did when I returned to the States was to call on Rachel. Her mother answered the door. Rachel no longer lived there. She had married a medical student she'd met in college. "I thought she wrote you." her mother said.

Her"Dear John" letter finally caught up with me while I was awaiting discharge. She gently explained the impossibility of a marriage between us. Looking back on it, I must have recovered rather quickly, although for the first few months I believed I didn't want to live. Like Rachel, I found someone else, whom I learned to love with a deep and permanent commitment that has lasted to this day.

Then, recently, after an interval of more than 40 years, I heard from Rachel again. Her husband had died. She was passing through town and had learned of my whereabouts through a mutual friend. We agreed to meet.

I felt both curious and excited. In the last few years, I hadn't thought about her, and her sudden call one morning had taken me aback. The actual sight of her was a shock. This white-haired matron at the restaurant table was the Rachel of my dreams and desires, the supple mermaid of that snapshot?

Yet time had given us a common reference and respect. We talked as old friends, and quickly discovered we were both grandparents.

"Do you remember this? " She handed me a slip of worn paper. It was a poem I'd written her while still in school. I examined the crude meter and pallid rhymes. Watching my face, she snatched the poem from me and returned it to her purse, as though fearful I was going to destroy it.

I told her about the snapshot, how I'd carried it all through the war.

"It wouldn't have worked out, you know." she said.

"How can you be sure? " I countered. "Ah, colleen, it might have been grand indeed—my Irish conscience and your Jewish guilt!"

Our laughter startled people at a nearby table. During the time left to us, our glances were furtive, oblique. I think that what we saw in each other repudiated what we'd once been to ourselves, we immortals.

Before I put her into a taxi, she turned to me. "I just wanted to see you once more. To tell you something." Her eyes met mine. "I wanted to thank you for having loved me as you did." We kissed, and she left.

From a store window my reflection stared back at me, an aging man, with gray hair stirred by an evening breeze. I decided to walk home. Her kiss still burned on my lips. I felt faint, and sat on a park bench. All around me the grass and trees were shining in the surreal glow of sunset. Something was being lifted out of me. Something had been completed, and the scene before me was so beautiful that I wanted to shout and dance and sing for joy.

That soon passed, as everything must, and presently I was able to stand and start for home.

最后一封信

The Last Relationship

佚名 / Anonymous

记得我们初次相识时，你好可爱。我们一起玩打仗，之后你骑到了我身上。

还记得我第一次邀请你和你弟弟来我家玩，开始你不想来，怕看到我的父母和兄弟。

我准备下楼时，你就扔爆米花，你躺在地上时，我折回来痛打了你一顿。

你上楼时，我正在玩风信旗。那时我就希望你能这么想——我可以和她玩风信旗吗？

再次遇见你是在情人节那天，我有一点儿害羞，不知道说什么好。

你坐在沙发上调电视频道时，我凝望着你，并希望你没有发现。

接着，我们静了下来，开始玩打仗。在打闹中你咬了我，我也咬了你，然后我们抱住了对方。

还记得初吻时，你在椅子上坐着，我在你面前站着。

然而，时间过得真快，你得走了，我在心里说："不，不要走！"

后来，在3月3日那天，你请求我做你的女朋友，我答应了，于是我们成了情侣。我希望我们的爱情之路顺利平坦。

我总记得那个星期天的晚上，你着实让我吃了一惊。你对我说："我爱你。"我问了你很多次，并要你别和我开玩笑了。最后，我还是回应了你："我也永远爱你。"

两个月后，你说你想离开我了。我对你说不要这样，冷静一下吧。这以后，我们又在一起了，但有时会发生争执。

大约在相识四个月后，我们计划出游一天，也就在那天，我们大吵了一架，之后就无话可说了。

终于，分手的那天到了。你骂我是泼妇，我气急败坏，起身离开。我站在墙后，祈祷着："上帝啊，别让这段感情就此结束。"

我的眼泪簌簌滑落，你走过来对我说："亲爱的，对不起，别哭了！"

我们一起回到家，你吻了我，我请你离开。

你交了新的朋友，与她们一同游玩。你不知道我是多么气愤，还有点儿忧伤。

于是，我终于告诉你，我们不再彼此需要了。

你却说让双方冷静一下，先分开一个月。可对我来说，这一个月就如两个月一样漫长。

后来，你给我打电话，说你很想我、爱我，也很需要我。

我们聊了一会儿，我的态度始终很冷淡。你又问我是否愿意回到你身边，我说一切已经无法挽回了。

之后，我写到，我和我深爱的男孩分手了，他走他的阳关道，我过我的独木桥。现在，我仍旧过得很好。

I remember the first time we met; you were as cute as can be and then we started to play fight then you sat on me.

You started to throw popcorn while I was going down the stairs and I came back to beat you up while you laid there.

I saw you again on Valentine's Day when I was a little shy, and didn't know what to say.

I remember the first time I asked you to come to my house with your brother; at first you didn't want to because of my mother, father, and brother.

When you came upstairs I was playing wit vane, I was hoping you were thinking—can I play with her?

While you were sitting on my couch changing channels on my TV, I was staring at you hoping you wouldn't catch me.

Then we became all cool and started to play fight, you bit me and I bit you, and then we held each other a little tight.

Then I remember our first kiss; you were sitting on the chair I was in front of you and stood there.

But the moment had to last and you had to go and in my mind I was saying, "No, he can't go!"

Then on March the 3rd you asked me to be your girl and I replied yes and we became a couple; I was hoping there would be no trouble.

I always remember on a Sunday night you surprised me and said, "I LOVE YOU." I asked you over and over and said don't play. I replied to you and said, "I love you too always."

Then two months past, you said you wanted to leave so I said don't worry just stay calm. So later on, we were going our way, but sometimes we had our bad days.

It was about our 4th month we had planned a day so we went out, but we had a big argument and didn't know what to say.

Then the date finally came. You called me a bitch, so I got up and walked away. I walked away and stood behind a wall then I just thought "God please don't let this relationship fall."

As a tear dropped from my eye, you walked by and said, "Baby I'm sorry, please don't cry."

So finally we went home and you kissed me and I told you to go.

You made new friends and went out and do you know I sat there pissed, mad, and a kind of blue.

So then I finally told you, you don't need me and I don't need you.

So you said let's just take a break 1 month, 2 months then I felt like it went away.

Then after a while you called me that you miss me, you love me and you want me.

We talked for a while, I was being cold then you asked me again and I explained myself and then said no.

So after that I wrote about a guy who stole my heart away as we said goodbye, he went his way and I went mine and here I am today.

一切都是从我的高中时代开始的，如今，我仍然惦念着我爱过的他。我不知道那是一种不成熟的爱，还是我的初恋，然而我明白，在我的心底，我依然无法将他忘怀。

最初，我们只是路友兼同学而已。我是高中一年级，他是二年级。在此之前，我们互不相识，然而，后来在公交车上，我坐在他的前面，他常常和我说话，并不断取笑我，这让我很生气。我经常说我恨他，可是后来……我背叛了自己的誓言。有一天，我最好的朋友想看看我日记本里写了些什么，我在公交车上将我写的内容读了出来，但是我没有注意到我憎恨的那个男孩和他的一群同伴就坐在我身后。他偷看了我写在日记本里的内容，那时，我急忙把本子放下，狠狠地盯着他。正在这个时候，坐在我前面的好友告诉我她读了我写的东西，说我在心里将爱情比喻为"沼泽"。听到这里，他站起来猛地将我的日记本抢走了。天哪！他大声地读着我写的内容，

怀旧的爱

My One and Only

佚名 / Anonymous

而日记里所写的全部是有关爱情的！上帝啊！我立刻尖叫着把我的东西抢了回来。我实在难以置信，因为他是我们学校最聪明的学生，也是学校的学生代表。停车后，我匆忙赶回家，我的脸颊害羞得直发热，通红通红的！那一刻，我知道我有点儿喜欢他了。

体育竞赛的日子来临了，他赢得了C组男生的第一名！哦，天哪！我为他奔跑的速度而惊叹，因为他常常夺得赛跑冠军，他跑得像风一样快。那天，我又对他多了一些感觉，我常常会把他写进我的日记里。然而大多数情况下他都不在学校，因为他要经常参加一些校际竞赛。

一次，因为实在太思念他，我竟然哭了起来。我多么盼望有一天他也会喜欢我。一天，当我听到有人说他喜欢我时，上帝呀，我几乎要晕过去了。人们都说我们会为了一点小事，如互相嘲笑而大费周张。因为我经常叫他"坚果钳"，这一称号让他很气愤。我经常嘲笑他由于那个时候，我非常调皮。一天，我决定请我的朋友用我所喜欢的德语写一封情书，因为我和他来自不同的国度。

朋友写好之后，我拿着这封情书让他在车上念给我听。他一边读，一边为我解释所写的内容，我知道情书的最后写的是"我爱你"。就在他读到最后，告诉我它的意思是"我爱你"时，我的脸颊红了。尽管我知道这

脸上有粉刺而使用洗面奶，全车的人听完之后哈哈大笑，他羞红了脸。一天，有谣言说我们都喜欢彼此！无论何时，我们在穿过街头时，也只是偶尔看看对方。然而我的心在他的热烈注视下怦怦直跳，我的心在颤抖。

并不是他写的，然而这似乎就是他的心声。

但是，并不是所有的爱情故事都有一个完美的结局。

有一天，我听别人说，他喜欢上了另一个女孩，我的心都要碎了。在公交车上，我曾故意说我已经交了一个男友，有意让他嫉妒，果不其然，他真的很是嫉妒。考试来临，我看到他正在门口等待一个女孩，我的心真的碎了。我哭了，因为他开始关注别的女孩了。在考试来临的前五天，他在车上告诉我他要回国了，天哪，我简直不敢相信自己的耳朵。最后一天，在校园里、在车上，我用自己的相机为他拍了照片。他下了车，我向他挥手告别……我无法相信，他离我而去了。

我想告诉你们的是，我们曾乘坐同一班汽车，在同一所学校学习，生于同一年。这一切简直就是莎士比亚笔下的《哈姆雷特》，我就是那个舞女，而他就是哈姆雷特。我永远不会忘记他，我的挚爱。他经常会梦到我，在梦里，他甚至还写了一首诗——《雨中吻》。我们都给彼此写着情诗，我为他写下一首诗，叫《只有你》，而他则为我写了《她是我的》。我仍然无法忘怀我们一起走过的那些开心的、让人难以忘怀的时光！唉，怀旧之情啊！……

It was all started when I was in high school, I still remember my love one. I am not sure if it is puppy love or first love, but I know deep inside my heart that I still remember him.

At first we were bus mates, and schoolmates too. I was in 1st year high school and he was in second. We still don't know each other before, but later on when I was sitting in front of him in the bus, he used to talk and tease me, which makes me angry with him. I used to say that I hate him but later on... I only eat my words. One day when my best friend wanted to see what I wrote in my diary, I was reading it in the bus and without noticing the guy whom I hate was sitting back of me with his buddies. He was peeping and reading the things that I wrote in the diary. I looked sharply at him and put the book down, then my friend who was in front of me that she has read what I wrote there that love is BOG, BOG, BOG in my heart. He was hearing it and suddenly without my knowledge he stood and snatched the diary from me! Whew! What he did was to read the book so loudly where everything was written there about love! Goodness! I was so shocked that I was screaming just to get it back. I couldn't believe it, because he's the most intelligent student in my school and he's the representative of our school too. Then after the bus dropped me to my house there I felt that I was so flushing hotly that my cheeks were so red! There, I realized that I have a crush on him!

Sports date came, and he was the champion for C group boys for running. Whew! Wow! I was really amazed when he runs, because he always come 1st in running and he runs like a wind. That day I felt more feelings for him. I used to write him always in my diary, but mostly he always went to another place because of interschool quiz.

I cried that time, because I was missing him so much, that I wish one day he'll like me too. Then one day I just heard that he likes me! My god, I nearly faint! Rumors spread that in the bus we always fights for simple things like teasing, because I use to call him NUTCRACKER which makes him so mad at me, and I always teased him for his pimples and about his using FACIAL cleanser which made my whole bus mates burst out laughing, and he was blushing, and then one fine day the rumors spread that we both are loving each other! Whenever we cross our paths we just look at each other casually, but my heart beats fast because he looks at me so intensely which makes my heart tremble.

I used to be always so naughty that time. One day I decided to ask my friend to write a love letter in language of German I loved, since we both are from different nations.

My friend wrote it, and in the bus I asked him to read the letter for me. He read it and explained what was written, and I know the last word written there was just I love you, but he told me that the last word means "I love you" which makes me blushed! Oh even though I know that he wasn't the one who wrote it, but it seems like he is telling it from his heart!

But not all the love story has happy ending...

One day, I heard that he likes another girl which makes my heart break! In the bus, I used to make him jealous of me by saying that I have a boyfriend. I made it, and he was jealous! Then examination came. I was really broken-heart when I saw him waiting for a girl in the gate! I cried, because of his caring for dating girl. Five days before the exam came, he told me in the bus that he's going to his country! My god! I can't believe it he's leaving me! The last day in the school and in the bus, I took a picture of him in my own camera! And when he went down in the bus I told bye... and then I still can't believe that he's gone.

To tell you we both are in the same bus, same school, we both are born on the same year. That was HAMLET! By Shakespeare I was the dancer, and he's Hamlet. I can never forget my one, my only one. He dreamed about me so many times! He even include the poem A KISS IN THE RAIN in his dream and we both composed a poem for each other, I composed a poem for him "ONLY YOU", and he composed a poem for me "SHE' S MINE". I still can't forget the happy unforgettable moments once we shared! Oh, nostalgia—

我的好妹妹
The Importance of Conscience

[英] 伊莱沙·M. 韦伯斯特 / Elisha M. Webster

一个抉择现在正困扰着我。正当我把洗好的衣服分别放进相应的卧室时，我不经意地看到了妹妹的日记本。妹妹今年 13 岁，她的日记本就像一个现代的潘多拉盒子深深地吸引着我。我该如何是好呢？过去，妹妹一直都是我妒忌的对象。我妒忌她迷人的微笑、可爱的个性，还有她的多才多艺，因为这些都挑战着我作为老大的地位。我私下偷偷地和她较劲，对她才能的憎恨更是与日俱增。我迫不及待地想把她的影子从我的个人成就上抹去。结果，我们平时很少说话。我寻找任何可以批评她的机会，并且急切地想要胜过她。现在，她的日记就在我的脚边，我根本没有考虑打开它的后果。我在意的既不是她的隐私权、我的行为道德，也不是她可能会受到的伤害。我仅仅是想从日记中发现一些罪证，来打破我的竞争者始终优秀的可能性。我把自己的坏念头归咎为姐姐的职责：检查她的言行举止是我的责任。如果尽不到义务，才是我的失误。

我犹豫不决地拨弄了几次地板上的日记本，最终还是打开了它。我快速地翻着书页，寻找着我的名字，确信一定能找到相应的证据。可是当我发现自己的名字时，脸一下子涨得通红。远比我想象得糟糕多了。我的脑袋一阵眩晕，瘫坐在了地板上。既没有阴谋也没有诽谤，日记中记录的仅仅是她对自己的简单陈述、她的人生目标和梦想，其中还有一个对她影响深远的人。我哭了起来。

我就是她心目中的英雄。她钦佩我的个性、我的成就，更具讽刺意味的是，还有我的正直。她想把我当成楷模。原来，这些年来她一直默默地观察我的选择和行为。我不再读了，结束了我的"罪行"。我花了太多的精力和她作对，而没有去好好地了解她。

这么多年来，我一直浪费时间来憎恨一个有魔力的人——并且现在还辜负了她对我的信任。是我自己失去了这么美好的东西，我下定决心再也不犯这样的错误。

看了妹妹日记中诚挚的语言后，裹在我心上的冰已经慢慢融化，我要重新去了解她。最终，我抛弃了那种不信任，正是它造成了我们之间的隔阂。在那个意义深远的下午，我把洗好的衣服放在一边，站起来准备去找她——这一次是去感受而不是责难，去拥抱而不是争执。无论如何，她是我的妹妹啊。

I was faced with a decision. While delivering laundry into the appropriate bedrooms, I stumbledupon my thirteen-year-old sister's diary, a modern-day Pandora's box, suffused with temptation. What was I to do? I had always been jealous of my little sister. Her charming smile, endearing personality and many talents threatened my place as leading lady. I competed with her tacitly and grew to resent her natural abilities. I felt it necessary to shatter her shadow with achievements of my own. As a result, we seldom spoke. I sought opportunities to criticize her and relished surpassing her acevements. Her diary lay at my feet, and I didn't think of the result of opening it. I considered not her privacy, the morality of my actions, nor her consequential pain. I merely savored the possibility of digging up enough dirt to soil my competitor's spotless record. I reasoned my iniquity as sisterly duty. It was my responsibility to keep a check on her activities. It would be wrong of me not to.

I tentatively plucked the book from the floor and opened it, fanning through the pages, searching for my name, convinced that I would discover scheming and slander. As I read, the blood ran from my face. It was worse than I suspected. I felt faint and slouched to the floor. There was neither conspiracy nor defamation. There was a succinct description of herself, her goals and her dreams followed by a short portrayal of the person who has inspired her most. I started to cry.

I was her hero. She admired me for my personality, my achievements and ironically, my integrity. She wanted to be like me. She had been watching me for years, quietly marveling over my choices and actions. I ceased reading, struck with the crime I had committed. I had expended so much energy into pushing her away that I had missed out on her.

I had wasted years resenting someone capable of magic—and now I had violated her trust. It was I who had lost something beautiful, and it was I who would never allow myself to do such a thing again.

Reading the earnest words, my sister had written seemed to melt an icy barrier around my heart, and I longed to know her again. I was finally able to put aside the petty insecurity that kept me from her. On that fateful afternoon, as I put aside the laundry and rose to my feet, I decided to go to her—this time to experience instead of to judge, to embrace instead of to fight. After all, she was my sister.

男人来自火星
女人来自金星

Whispering
Love

[美] 约翰·格雷 / John Gray

设想男人是从火星上来的，女人是从金星上来的。

很久以前的一天，火星人用望远镜眺望远方时，发现了金星人，这匆匆一瞥把火星人心中沉睡的感情唤醒了。他们对这种感情从不知晓。坠入爱河的火星人很快发明了太空旅行，飞往金星。金星上的女人们张开双臂迎接他们的到来。火星男人与金星女人之间的爱情真是奇妙。他们一起愉快地生活，一起工作，同甘共苦，他们都忘了彼此是来自不同的星球，忘了本应具有的差异。一天早晨，火星人和金星人完全忘却了彼此的不同，也就是从那天起，冲突开始在男人与女人之间发生。

女人抱怨男人最多的是男人不会倾听。当女人说话时，男人不是完全不理睬，就是稍听片刻，掂量一下困扰女人的问题，然后自傲地抛给女人一个解决的办法以安慰她就算了事。无论女人抱怨了多少次，说他没有倾听，他就是不懂，依然故技重演。女人需要同情，可男人以为她需要的是解决办法。

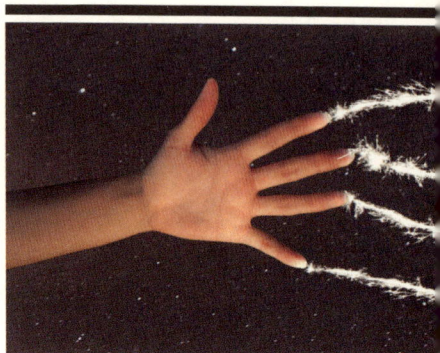

男人最常抱怨女人总试图改造自己。女人爱上男人时，便觉得帮助他成长是自己的责任，并尽力想帮助男人改进做事的方式。女人成立了家庭促进会，而改进男人就是它的首要目标。无论男人怎样拒绝她的帮助，女人都一再坚持，伺机帮助他或是告诉他该做什么。女人认为自己是在调教男人，而男人却觉得自己被控制了。男人崇尚权力、个人能力和成功。他们本是以取得成功的能力作为给自己的定义的。对他们而言，实现目标举足轻重，因为这能证明他们自身

的能力，会让他们有良好的感觉。而男人
要想建立良好的自我感觉，就必须独立自
主地取得种种成功。在男人看来，女人自
作主张提出的建议就是认为他们不知道该
做什么，不能凭独自的力量获取胜利。

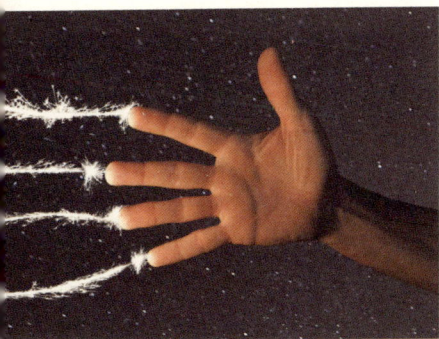

他们对此很恼火，因为个人能力对于他们非
常重要。然而，如果男人确实需要帮助，取
得帮助也是明智之举。在这种情况下，他会
和一位他所敬重的人谈论自己的困难。男人
谈论困难就是请求他人提供建议。被请求的
人因此会颇感荣幸，并顺其自然地抒发感想，
听对方诉说，然后提供宝贵的建议。男人的
这种习惯，在一定程度上导致了他们在倾听
女人谈论自己的情感和困惑时，本能地提供
解决方案。

女人却对这些不予重视。她们是在感情和与人相处的融洽程度，以及交流中确定自我感觉的。女人在诉说感情和彼此联系中获得满足。交流对于她们至关重要，分担私人感情比达到目的要重要得多，让她们获得满足感的巨大源泉之一就是交谈与联系。男人看重的是目的，女人看重的是关系。她们更注重表达善意、友爱和关怀。女人具有敏锐的直觉，能处处为他人的需求和情感着想是她们引以为豪的事。主动向同伴提供帮助被她们看成是伟大的爱的展示。女人不洞悉男人的天性，就很容易在不知不觉中伤害了自己所挚爱的男人。

爱情神奇而微妙，只有记住男女之间的差异，爱情才会持久。

Imagine that men are from Mars and women are from Venus.

One day, long ago, the Martians, looking through their telescopes, discovered the Venusians. Just glimpsing the Venusians awakened feelings they had never known. They fell in love and quickly invented space travel and flew to Venus. The Venusians welcomed the Martians with open arms. The love between the Venusians and Martians was magical. They delighted in being together, doing things together and sharing together. Both the Martians and Venusians forgot that they were from different planets, and were supposed to be different. And one morning, everything they had learned about their differences was erased from their memory. And since that day, men and women have been in conflict.

The most frequently expressed complaint women have about men is that men don't listen. Either a man completely ignores her when she speaks, or he listens for a few beats, assesses what's bothering her, and then he proudly puts on his Mr. Fix-it hat, and offers her a solution to make her feel better. No matter how many times she tells him that he's not listening, he doesn't get it, and he keeps doing the same thing. She wants sympathy, he thinks she wants solutions.

The most frequently expressed complaint men have about women is that women are always trying to change them. When a woman loves a man, she feels responsible to assist him in growing and tries to help him improve the way he does things. She forms the Home Improvement Committee, and he becomes her primary focus. No matter how much he resists her help, she persists, waiting for an opportunity to help him or to tell him what to do. She thinks she's nurturing him, while he feels he's being controlled. Martians value power, competency, efficiency, and achievement. Their sense of self is defined through their ability to achieve results. Achieving goals is very important to a Martian, because it's the way for him to prove his competence and thus feel good about himself. And for him to feel good about himself, he must achieve these goals alone, by himself. To offer a man unsolicited advice is to presume that he doesn't know what to do or that he can't do it on his own.

Men are very touchy about this, because the issue of competence is so very important to them. However, if he truly does need help, then it's a sign of wisdom to get it. In this case, he'll find someone he respects and then talk about his problem. Talking about a problem on Mars is an invitation for advice. Another Martian feels honored by the opportunity. Automatically, he puts on his Mr.Fix-it hat, listens for a few beats, and then offers some jewels of advice. This Martian custom is one of the reasons men instinctively offer solutions when a woman talks about her feelings or about her problems.

Venusians have different values. Their sense of self is defined through their feelings and the quality of their relationships and their communication. They experience fulfillment through sharing and relating. Communication is of primary importance. To share their personal feelings is much more important than achieving goals or success. Talking and relating to one another is a source of tremendous fulfillment. Instead of being goal-oriented, women are relationship-oriented. They are more concerned with expressing their goodness, their love, their caring. Venusians are very intuitive. They pride themselves on being considerate of the needs and feelings of others. A sign of great love is to offer help and assistance to another Venusian without even being asked. Without this insight into the nature of men, it's very easy for a woman to unknowingly and unintentionally hurt and offend the man she loves most.

Love is magical, and it can last if we remember our differences.

爱因难而美好

Love Is Difficult

［美］勒内·马利亚·里尔克 / Rainer Maria Rilke

Love Is Difficult

爱是一件美好的事情：因为爱是艰难的。一个人去爱另一个人，这也许是神给予我们的最艰难、最重大的任务，是最后的考验与测试，是最崇高的工作，别的工作都不过是为此而作的准备。所以，那些一切都还刚刚开始的青年还不能去爱，他们必须要学习去爱。必须用他们整个生命，用一切力量，用积聚了他们寂寞、痛苦和荣誉感的心去学习爱。在学习这个长久而专注的过程中，

爱就会永远地铭刻心间——在深深的寂寞中孤独地等待，是为了所爱的人。爱的要义并不是什么倾心、献身或两人的结合（那会是怎样的一种结合呢？是一种糊涂的、不负责任的、轻率的结合）。它对于个人是一种崇高的动力，是变成熟并实现自身的完善，去完成一

个世界，是为了另一个人而完成一个自己的世界，这是一个艰巨的、不可妥协的目标，用坚定的信念，召唤其走向更广阔的空间。青年们应把爱当成他们的课业、他们工作的意义，并在其中

（"昼夜不停地探索、锤炼"）去面对那些给予他们的爱。至于倾心、献身，以及结合，还不是他们所能做的（他们还需长时间地克制和积累），那是最后的终点，也许是我们现在还几乎不能达到的境界。

It is also good to love: because love is difficult. For one human being to love another human being: that is perhaps the most difficult task that has been entrustedto us, the ultimate task, the final test and proof, the work for which all other work is merely preparation. That is why young people, who are beginners in everything, are not yet capable of love: it is something they must learn. With their whole being, with all their forces, gathered around their solitary, anxious, upward-beating heart, they must learn to love. But learning-time is always a long, secludedtime ahead and far on into life, is solitude, a heightened and deepened kind of aloneness for the person who loves. Loving does not at first mean merging, surrendering, and uniting with another person (for what would a union be of two people who are unclarified, unfinished, and still incoherent). It is a high inducement for the individual to ripen, to become something in himself, to become world, to become world in himself for the sake of another person; it is a great, demanding claim on him, something that chooses him and calls him to vast distances. Only in this sense, as the task of working on themselves ("to hearken and to hammer day and night"), may young people use the love that is given to them. Merging and surrendering and every kind of communion is not for them (who must still, for a long, long time, save and gather themselves) it is the ultimate, is perhaps that for which human lives are as yet barely large enough.

用虔诚的爱来
迎接今天
I Will Greet This Day with
Love in My Heart

[英] 奥格·曼迪诺 / Og Mandino

我要用虔诚的爱来迎接今天。因为，这是一切冒险事业得以成功的最大秘诀。强力可以劈开盾牌，甚至摧毁生命，只有无形的爱的力量，才能打开人们的心扉。我要让爱成为我最强大的无人可敌的武器。

我该做些什么呢？自此，我将充满爱心地对待一切，使自己重获新生。我爱阳光，它能温暖我的体魄；我爱雨水，它能净化我的心灵；我爱光明，它能照亮我前进的道路；我也爱黑夜，它使我看到星辰。我将迎接快乐，它使我心胸开阔。我将忍受悲伤，它使我灵魂开启。我将接受我应得的报酬，我也将不惧给我以挑战的艰险。

我该说些什么呢？我歌颂敌人，于是他们成为我的朋友；我鼓励朋友，于是我们情同手足。我要常找些理由去赞美别人，而绝不绞尽脑汁寻找借口搬弄是非。愤怒得忍不住要批评别人时，咬住舌头；激动得禁不住要赞美别人时，就大声说出口。

鸟儿、风儿、海浪以及世间的万物不都在用它们美妙悦耳的歌声赞美它们的造物主吗？我为什么不用同样的歌声去赞美它们的儿女呢？从此，我要记住这一秘诀，它能改变我的生活。

我该如何行动呢？我要把爱奉献给所有的人，因为每个人都有令人钦佩的优秀品质，虽然有时不易察觉。我要用爱击垮阻碍人们心灵自由沟通的怀疑与仇恨之墙，同时，我要用我的爱在人们之间搭建一座桥梁，使我的爱能自如地进驻他们的灵魂。

我爱雄心勃勃的人，因为他们能激励我！我爱失败者，因为他们能教育我。我爱王侯，他们也是凡人。我爱弱者，他们也是天才。我爱富人，他们更寂寞。

我爱贫者，因为贫者甚多。我爱少年，因为他们纯真。我爱长者，因为他们睿智。我爱貌美的人，因为他们有忧郁的眼神。我爱丑陋的人，因为他们有颗平静的心。

我该对他们的行为做出怎样的反应呢？爱吧。因为爱不仅是开启人们心灵的钥匙，而且也是抵挡仇恨之箭与愤怒之矛的盾牌。有了爱，即使逆境与挫折如锋利的长矛攻击我的新盾，也都会变得如细雨般温柔。

我该如何面对与我不期而遇的每个人呢？只有一种办法，就是默默地祝福他，并说"我爱你"。那闪现在我的眼神中的无言的爱，会舒展我紧锁的眉头，让我会心的微笑攀至嘴角，在我的声音中回荡。于是，他将向我敞开心扉。
……

I will greet this day with love in my heart. For this is the greatest secret of success in all ventures. Muscle can split a shield and even destroy life but only the unseen power of love can open the hearts of men. I will make love my greatest weapon and no one can defend against its force.

And how will I do this? Henceforth will I look on all things with love and I will be born again. I will love the sun for it warms my bones; yet I will love the rain for it cleanses my spirit. I will love the light for it shows me the way; yet I will love the darkness for it shows me the stars. I will welcome happiness for it enlarges my heart; yet I will endure sadness for it opens my soul. I will acknowledge rewards for they are my due; yet I will welcome obstacles for they are my challenge.

And how will I speak? I will laud my enemies and they will become friends; I will encourage my friends and they will become brothers. Always will I dig for reasons to applaud; never will I scratch for excuses to gossip. When I am tempted to criticize I will bite on my tongue; when I am moved to praise I will shout from the roofs.

Is it not so that birds, the wind, the sea and all nature speaks with the music of praise for their creator? Cannot I speak with the same music to his children? Henceforth will I remember this secret and it will change my life.

And how will I act? I will love all manner of men for each has qualities to be admired even though they be hidden. With love I will tear down the wall of suspicion and hate which they have built round their hearts and in its place will I build bridges so that my love may enter their souls.

I will love the ambitious for they can inspire me! I will love the failures for they can teach me. I will love the kings for they are but human.I will love the meek for they are divine. I will love the rich for they are yet lonely.

I will love the poor for they are so many. I will love the young for the faith they hold I will love the old for the wisdom they share. I will love the beautiful for their eyes of sadness I will love the ugly for their souls of peace.

But how will I react to the actions of others? With love. For just as love is my weapon to open the hearts of men, love is also my shield to repulse the arrows of hate and the spears of anger. Adversity and discouragement will beat against my new shield and become as the softest of rains.

And how will I confront each whom I meet? In only one way. In silence and to myself I will address him and say "I Love You". Though spoken in silence these words will shine in my eyes, unwrinkled my brow, bring a smile to my lips, and echo in my voice; and his heart will be opened.

...

友谊之树常青

How to Heal a Friendship

佚名 / Anonymous

初三时，杰西卡和乔侬丝是最好的朋友，两人形影不离。有一天，两人闹矛盾，乔侬丝不再和杰西卡说话了。三个多月来，乔侬丝都不和杰西卡说话，也不回她的纸条。"那个时候，我才发现，她对我多么重要，"杰西卡说，"我甚至无法集中精神学习，一心想着如何修复我们的友谊。"

第二个学期，杰西卡再次努力尝试。这次，乔侬丝也愿意澄清误会。经过一段时间的努力，友谊终于恢复了。

很多人都经受过友谊破裂所带来的痛苦，可喜的是，大部分友谊都能修复如初。

最近，牛津大学教授麦克·阿尔盖尔完成了一项长达 15 年的探索人类快乐缘由的研究。这项研究的发现是什么呢？快乐的关键在于拥有一个知己和一群朋友。另一项研究表明，社会关系能让我们活得更加健康，承受更大的压力。因此，维持一份健康长久的友谊是值得我们付出努力的！

如果你想要修复一份破裂的友谊，可以尝试下面的建议。

未经证实之前，假设你的朋友是无辜的。

我们很容易作最坏的打算。如果朋友伤害了你，他可能并没有意识到自己对你的伤害。美国一个博士生麦特先生，回想起了两段因言语尖锐而导致的友谊破裂。不过，不久后，两份友谊都得到了修复。

"如果有人伤害了你，或许让他们知道这个情况会更好些，"麦特说，"事实上，我们都是普通人，通常也会把事情搞砸。你必须给予别人充分的信任，因为你也会同样需要这份信任。"

主动和你的朋友沟通。

一旦受到伤害，你本能的反应可能就是马上离开以保护自己，如果这样做的话，你们的友谊可能就随之结束了。

"你要主动和朋友沟通，"20 岁的雅美说，她曾经挽救了多份破裂的友谊，"彼此一旦失去信任，友谊也就破碎了。朋友之间都要主动伸出手来，要证明自己是值得对方信赖的。"

主动向对方表示歉意。

即便是你受到伤害，也应该为自己做的错事道歉。不要去证明自己是对的，否则，原有的矛盾都无法解决。

共同坦然面对误会。

试着站在朋友的立场来看问题，敞开心扉，和和气气地讨论问题。刚开始，杰西卡不明白乔依丝为什么不和自己说话，后来，乔依丝终于解释说，杰西卡的嘲弄让她很烦闷。"我终于发现，她生气是因为我在班上男生面前取笑了她。"杰西卡解释道。她以为自己的逗弄没什么，不会伤害到乔依丝。但是，当她知道这样做令乔依丝很难堪后，就不再这样，她们也就和好如初了。

妮可儿和米雪从幼儿园开始就是好朋友了。到了大学，两人的关系有了微妙变化，米雪开始和妮可儿保持距离了。"很长一段时间彼此没有说话了，之后，我试着和解，"妮可儿说，"但是，我们现在好像成了客套的熟人了。"

友谊会起变化是很正常的事，两个朋友往往会慢慢疏远。当其中一人试图维系，而另一个打算放弃的时候，友谊就出现问题了。

如果你的朋友不愿意重归于好，那就接受这个事实，继续自己的生活吧。但是，如果你有能力修复，那么，你就会拥有这样一份友谊——牢固而又真挚。

Jessica and Joyce were best friends in junior grade three. They did almost everything together. Then one day, after a misunderstanding, Joyce stopped talking to Jessica. For more than three months, Joyce refused to talk to Jessica or answer her notes. "During that time, I found out what an important friend she was," Jessica says,"I couldn't even concentrate when I was studying, l just thought about how to mend our friendship."

The next semester, Jessica tried again. This time, Joyce was willing to work it out. It took some time and effort, but the friendship was healed.

Most of us have suffered the pain of broken friendships. But the good news is that most friendships can be mended.

Oxford professor Michael Argyle recently finished a 15-year study that explored what makes people happy. What did he find? The key to happiness is having one close relationship and a network of friends. Other studies show that our social connections make us healthier and more resilient to stress. Maintaining long-lasting, healthy friendship is worth the effort!

If there's a broken friendship you'd like to mend, try the following advice.

Give your friend the benefit of the doubt.

It's easy to assume the worst. But if a friend has hurt you, he may not even realize he's done so. Matt, an American doctoral student, remembers two friendships broken by hurtful words. Both relationships were later healed.

"It's probably true that if someone hurts you, they should have known better," Matt says, "but the fact is we are all human and we mess things up. You need to give people the benefit of the doubt because you will need that, as well."

Take the initiative to communicate with your friend.

If you've been hurt, your instinct is probably to pull away and protect yourself. But if you do this, the friendship will likely die.

"You need to reach out," says 20-year-old Jamie, who has restored several broken friendships, "Friendships get broken when trust is lost. Both friends need to reach out and demonstrate they are trustworthy. "

Be the first to apologize.

Even if you were hurt, apologize for anything you did wrong. Give up your right to be proven right. Otherwise the conflict won't be forgotten, as it should be.

Walk through the conflict together.

Start by trying to see things from your friend's point of view. Talk about the problems openly but kindly. At first, Jessica didn't understand why Joyce stopped talking to her. Then Joyce finally explained that Jessica's teasing bothered her. "I finally found out she was angry because I teased her in front of the boys in our class. " Jessica explained. Jessica meant nothing by her teasing and thought it shouldn't bother Joyce. But when she accepted that it was embarrassing to Joyce, she stopped. Then their friendship could heal.

Nicole and Michelle had been best friends since preschool. But in college, Michelle suddenly pulled away. "We didn't talk to each other for a while, then tried to reconcile," Nicole says, "But we're just polite acquaintances now. "

It's normal for friendships to change. Often two friends just drift apart. Problems come when one friend tries to hang on while the other friend lets go.

If your friend isn't willing to work things out, accept it and move on. But if you are able to reconcile, you'll have a friendship that's tried-and-true!

丢掉爱的

The 记分卡
Scorecard

佚名 /Anonymous

我们在电影演完后，开始闲聊起来。温暖的炉火，圣诞的彩灯，家人的笑声，这一切使我满意地笑了。这时，母亲说："谁想去……"母亲的话还没说完，整个屋子就没人了，比输了足球赛的看台空得还快。

房间里只剩下我和我的男友托德。他满脸困惑，问我是怎么回事。我看看笑着的母亲，对他说："让我们准备去给母亲的汽车加油吧。"

他马上回答说："外边冰天雪地，而且，现在已经是夜里十一点半了。"我笑了笑说："那你最好穿上大衣，戴上手套。"

我们迅速地擦掉挡风玻璃上的霜，一起进入车内。在去加油站的途中，托德让我解释为什么要在这样的天气、这么晚的夜里给妈妈的车加油。我咯咯地笑着说："每次我们兄弟姐妹回来过节，都要帮爸爸为妈妈的车加油。我们把它看成一项游戏，我们能猜到妈妈什么时候让我们去，最后留在房间里的人要去为她的车加油。"

"你一定是在和我开玩笑。"托德说。

"我没有和你开玩笑。"我说。

在加油站的人给车加油的时候，我搓着手，蹦跳着让自己感觉暖和一点儿。"我还是不明白，你妈妈为什么不自己来做？"托德问。

我微笑着说："我知道这听起来有点儿荒唐，我给你解释一下吧。我妈妈二十多年没有自己加过油，总是由我爸爸代劳。"托德很困惑地问："你爸爸是否厌烦过？"我摇着头，简单地回答说："不，他从未抱怨过。"

"真是难以想象。"托德立即回答道。

"不，真的不会。"我耐心地解释，"大学二年级我回家度假的时候，认为什么事情都懂了，尤其认为女人应该独立自主。一天晚上，母亲和我包装礼品时，我对她说，等我结婚了，一定要让我的丈夫帮我打扫房间、洗衣服、做饭，什么家务活他都得干。我还问她，整天洗洗涮涮烦不烦。令我不能相信的是，她说她很乐意做这些事情。我就告诉她这是九十年代了，要男女平等。

"妈妈平静地听我说完，在一件礼物上系完一条丝带后，看着我的眼睛，坚定地说：'亲爱的，总会有你明白的那天的。'

"她的话使我更生气，更疑惑，于是我要求她解释明白。母亲笑了，开始给我解释：

"'在婚姻生活当中，有些事是你想干的，有些事是你不愿意干的。你们可以挑出愿意为对方干的事，从而共同承担生活的责任。我挺喜欢洗衣服的，虽然会花很多时间，我还是愿意为你爸爸做这些事情。但是，我不喜欢去给车加油，汽油的味道让我恶心，尤其是在冬天，天气寒冷，我更不喜欢出去，所以你爸爸总是替我干这件事情。还有，你爸爸去杂货店买东西，我做饭；你爸爸割草，我清理。当然，这样的分工还很多。'

"'你知道吗？'妈妈继续说，'婚姻当中没有记分卡，你为对方做一些事情，会使他生活得轻松。你不会厌倦为自己心爱的人洗衣服、做饭或干其他的事情，因为你爱他，你做的一切都出自对他的爱。'

"这些年来我一直考虑妈妈的话，她对婚姻有很深的理解。我羡慕爸爸妈妈相亲相爱，而且，我结婚了，也不要记分卡。"

托德在回家的路上，罕见的安静。到家后，他关掉发动机，转向我，带着温暖地微笑着，目光闪烁，捧起我的手，非常温柔地对我说："我随时准备为你的车去加油。"

As the movie came to an end the room filled with chatter. The warm fire, twinkling Christmas lights and laughter from family brought a contented smile to my face. The minute Mom said, "Who wants..."the room emptied quicker than the stands at a losing football game.

My boyfriend Todd and I were the only ones left. With a bewildered look on his face he asked me what just happened. Catching the laughter on my mom's face, I said to Todd, "We are going to go put gas in my mom's car."

He quickly replied, "It's freezing out there, and it's almost 11:30 P.M." Smiling, I said, "Then you had better your coat and gloves."

After hurriedly chipping the frost off the windshield, we bundled into the car. On the way to the gas station, Todd asked me to explain why in the world we were going to get my mom gas so late at night. Chuckling, I said, "When my siblings and I come home for the holidays, we help my dad get gas for my mom. It has turned into a game with all of us. We can tell when at mom is going to ask and the last one in the room has to go."

"You have got to be kidding me!" Todd responded.

"There is no getting out of it." I said.

While pumping the gas, we clapped our hands and jumped around to stay warm. "I still don't get it. Why doesn't your mom put the gas in the car herself ? "Todd asked.

With mirth in my eyes, I said, " I know it sounds insane, but let me explain. My mom has not pumped gas in over two decades. My dad always pumps gas for her. "With a confused look, Todd asked if my dad was ever annoyed with having to pump gas for his wife all the time. Shaking my head, I simply said, "No, he has never complained."

"That's crazy."Todd quickly replied.

"No, not really." I explained patiently. "When I came home for the holidays my sophomore year of college, I thought I knew everything. I was on this big female independence kick. One evening, my mom and I were wrapping presents, and I told her that when I got married, my husband was going to help clean, do laundry, cook, the whole bit. Then I asked her if she ever got tired of doing the laundry and dishes. She calmly told me it did not bother her. This was difficult for me to believe. I began to give her a lecture about this being the 90s, and equality between the sexes.

"Mom listened patiently. Then after setting the ribbon aside, she looked me square in the eyes. 'Someday, dear, you will understand. '

"This only irritated me more. I didn't understand one bit. And so I demanded more of an explanation. Mom smiled, and began to explain:

" 'In a marriage, there are some things you like to do and some things you don't. So, together, you figure out what little things you are willing to do for each other. You share the responsibilities. I really don't mind doing the laundry. Sure, it takes some time, but it is something I do for your dad. On the other hand, I do not like to pump gas. The smell of the fumes bothers me. And I don't like to stand out in the freezing cold. So, your dad always puts gas in my car. Your dad grocery shops, and I cook. Your dad mows the grass, and I clean. I could go on and on. '

" 'You see,' my mother continued, 'in marriage, there is no scorecard.

You do little things for each other to make the other's life easier. If you think of it as helping the person you love, you don't become annoyed with doing the laundry or cooking, or any task, because you' re doing it out of love. '

"Over the years, I have often reflected on what my mom said. She has a great perspective on marriage. I like how my mom and dad take care of each other. And you know what? One day, when I'm married, I don't want to have a scorecard either."

Todd was unusually quiet the rest of the way home. After he shut off the engine, he turned to me and took my hands in his with a warm smile and a twinkle in his eye. "Anytime you want, "he said in a soft voice, "I'll pump gas for you."

淘气的天使。

WHY I TEACH

[英] 惠特尼·L. 葛拉德 / Whitney L. Gra

我很了解我的学生们。在我们乡村中学里，每天都会有一群七年级的学生，背着双肩背包，沿着走廊的瓷砖地板一边嚷嚷，一边慢悠悠地从一间教室走到另一间教室。我站在教室门口看着他们，就像一个将军在阅兵似的。我为能叫出他们每一个人的名字而感到高兴。

我知道他们的秘密以及他们的故事。多拉是一个懒散而害羞的女孩，我知道这是因为她在家的时候不愿太惹人注意，以免因闯祸而遭到继父的殴打；杰伊可以像一个十年级的学生那样投掷棒球，当他顶着一头金黄色的头发大摇大摆地走过时，所有女孩都欣喜若狂，但是我知道他对棒球根本没兴趣，只是不敢违抗父命而已，与女孩子出去约会也会让他感到害怕；孩子们都认为基思只是班上的小丑，但是我知道他梦想能成为一名宇航员，所以我把他推荐给了一个太空夏令营。我了解我的学生们，因为我是他们的写作老师。他们信任我，并告诉我他们的故事，所以我有了与他们每一个人分享秘密的特权。

我教给我的学生们文字的力量，尝试着让他们通过写作来释放自己，表达自己。在写作课上，我们学着相互信任，因为我们知道公开而诚实地写作是多么困难，我们学着鼓足勇气来分享我们的语言。在教室里，我们每天都可以看到勇气，我总会为学生们的心里话而感到震惊。

一个有关勇气的例子发生在"作家工作室"中的一个自愿分享作品的环节中。学校里来了一个名叫阿尔的新学生，他很瘦小，一张娃娃脸上还有两个小酒窝，这让他看起来比其他同学都小。

事实上，当阿尔在两周前第一次来到班上时，一个同学就说："你不该在七年级，你还是个孩子呢！"

阿尔立即回答道："我叫阿尔·比尔史灵顿，我上七年级。"

尽管他的勇气可嘉，可毕竟刚来到我们中间，仍然处于适应阶段。所以，当他自愿要在"作家工作室"上朗读自己的作文时，我感到很惊讶。像往常一样，我笑着点头示意他开始朗读，心里也在为他默默地祈祷，希望其他同学不要在他朗读之后取笑他。教室陷入了沉寂，阿尔开始朗读了。

"如果说我有一个愿望，那就是可以见到爸爸……"他的声音洪亮而清晰。在朗读的大约 15 分钟里，他引起了我那些通常不安分的七年级学生的注意。他讲述了自己从未见过父亲的原因：当他还是个小孩时，父亲就离开了家。他和大家分享了一些他的秘密。

他如此小的年龄就要为成为家里唯一的男子汉而努力，割草，修理损坏的下水道。他投给我们一种思想：他的脑海里满是他的父亲在哪里，以及他为什么离开的疑问。

我环顾教室四周，寻找着班级里窃笑的面孔。我知道这些学生喜欢取笑别人，但是此时没有一个窃笑者，没有四处张望，没有不耐烦的表情，也没有要攻击的架势。同学们都在听着，确实在听。他们都望着阿尔，像海绵吸水一样倾听着他的话语。我感到很欣慰。

阿尔继续朗读着，叙述着他的梦魇，叙述他自己从未感觉到做一个男子汉对自己是如此重要，可这离自己又太遥远了。当他朗读着如此深情而真诚的话语时，我可以听出他的声音在颤抖，我看到他那有着两个酒窝的脸颊上淌下了一滴泪珠。我看了一下观众，杰西卡和其他几个少数静静倾听的同学也是泪眼蒙眬。

我想，他们允许他这样做，允许他分享一些或许他从来没有与别人分享过的东西，而且他们没有歧视或取笑他，我哽咽了。

在结尾的时候，阿尔竭力朗读着最后一句话："如果说我有一个愿望的话，那就是能见到我的爸爸，这样我就不

会……"他的泪水已经决堤了，我们也是。"……这样我就不会每天晚上躺在床上想象他的样子了。"

在我没有作出任何暗示的情况下，全体同学起立为他鼓掌。当大家纷纷跑上前去拥抱他的时候，阿尔笑了。

这就是我之所以教书的原因。之所以教书，是因为我可以在那些面孔下面了解到一些故事，是因为我可以看着孩子们成长、欢笑、学习和友爱，更是因为那些像阿尔一样的学生。

I know my students. Masses of awkward seventh graders swarm the halls of my rural middle school each day, hauling backpacks over one shoulder, talking and shuffling along the tile hallway floor from class to class. I watch them like a general from my post, my classroom door, and smile at the fact that I can call each one by name.

I know their secrets, their stories. Dora slouches and is shy, and I know it is because she spends all her time at home trying not to get noticed, so she won't feel the brunt of her stepfather's angry hand. Jay can pitch like a tenth grader, and all the girls swoon when he and his blond hair strut by, but I know he doesn't really even like baseball that much he plays because his dad wants him to and he is too scared to ask out the girl he likes. The kids think Keith is just the class clown, but I know of his dreams to become an astronaut and I've recommended him for space camp. I know my students because I am their writing teacher. They trust me with their stories and so I am given the privilege of having a secret bond with each and every one of them.

I teach my students about the power of words, and I try to let them find release and expression through writing. We learn to trust each other in writing class because we learn how hard it is to write openly and honestly, and we learn that sharing your words takes courage. I see courage every day in my classroom, and I am always amazed at the words that come from my students' hearts.

One such example of courage took place during author's chair, a sharing session at the end of our writer's workshop in which students volunteer to share what they have written. We had a new student to the school, Al. Al was small and, with his dimpled cheeks and baby face, he looked younger than his classmates.

In fact, when Al was first introduced to the class two weeks earlier, one student said,"You're not in the seventh grade. You're a baby. "

To that, Al quickly responded, "I'm Al Billslington, and I am in the seventh grade. "

Despite his obvious courage, Al had been with us for only a short while and was still trying to fit in. So I was a little surprised when he volunteered to read during author's chair. I had one of those teacher moments, when I smiled and nodded for him to read, while inside I said a silent prayer that the other students would not tease the new kid after he read. The room fell silent, and Al began to read.

"If I had one wish, it would be to meet my dad... " He started out loud and clear and held the attention of my usually restless seventh graders as he read on for what seemed like fifteen minutes. He told of how he had never known his father, who had left the family when Al was a baby.

He shared the intimate details of his struggles to be the only man in the house at such a young age, of having to mow the lawn and fix broken pipes. He revealed to us the thoughts that raced through his mind constantly about where his father might be and why he might have left.

My eyes scanned the room for snickering faces of seventh-grade kids who I knew were prone to jump at a weakness and try to crack a joke, but there were no snickers. There were no rolling eyes or gestures insinuating boredom or pending attacks. All of my seventh-grade students were listening, really listening. Their eyes were on Al, and they were absorbing his words like sponges. My heart was full.

Al continued on, telling of nightmares at night, of never knowing a man so important to him, yet so unreal. I could hear his voice growing shaky as he read such passionate and honest words, and I saw a tear roll down one of his dimpled cheeks. I looked to the audience. There were tears on Jessica's face and on the faces of a few others seated quietly, intently listening.

They are letting him do this, I thought. They are allowing him to share something he perhaps has never shared before, and they aren't judging him or teasing him. I felt a lump in my own throat.

Al finished, struggling now to read his last sentence. "If I had one wish, it would be to meet my dad, so I wouldn't... " His tears were rolling now, and so were ours, "... so I wouldn't have to close my eyes in bed every night just wondering what he looks like. "

Without any cue from me, the class stood up and applauded. Al smiled from ear to ear as they all rushed him with hugs. I was floored.

This is why I teach. I teach because I am allowed to learn the stories behind the faces. I teach because I can watch kids grow and laugh and learn and love. I teach because of students like Al.

承载着爱与思念的手表
Mother's Watch

[美]雷蒙德·巴里 / Raymond Barry

放在精美礼品盒里的是一块镶有 17 颗宝石的"爱而近"牌表，那是我的母亲在 1916 年 9 月结婚前买的。那块表极具时代感，功能齐全又有装饰作用——对于当时的女性而言，那是一件非常珍贵的饰物。当你按一下发条钮，小盒就会弹开，表盘便随之露出。在我十三四岁时，母亲将那块表送给我，我让人把它改造成了一块手表。对我而言，那仅仅是另一件属于我的物品。1941 年 4 月，我离家参军时，带走了那块表。

我们的部队被派往菲律宾群岛。在横渡太平洋的海船上，我很粗心，在洗澡时将表系在吃水线上，险些丢掉。幸运的是，一位好心的美国兵发现了它，并将其归还于我。当时，那块表对我来说只是一件物品。除此之外，似乎再没有什么特别之处了。

空袭珍珠港之后，我们退到巴丹半岛。我开始关注我的手表了。敌军如此临近，我将母亲给我的手表带在身边真是笨极了。当我们被告知要向日本投降时，我意识到我的手表可能会成为日本人的战利品。我不忍将其扔进丛林，又不想其落入敌军之手，我想靠智慧骗过逮捕人员。我将表拴在左脚踝上，用袜子盖上。为了加强保护，我又穿了一双护腿。想不到的是，从此我开始了一场长达34个月之久的"藏表"游戏。

我们的部队投降了，被迫进入臭名昭著的"巴丹死亡行军"。我用带子将表裹住，塞入短裤的小表袋里。一天，我被遣往吕宋岛北部进行分队劳作，在一辆卡车的后斗里，我被一个始终都不离开的日本兵看守着。他的眼睛恰好看到了我小口袋的鼓包。他伸出一只带着手套的手摸了一下鼓包。我整个人都僵住了，屏住呼吸，恐怕会失去这件现今已很珍贵的物品。令人惊奇的是，守卫并没有好奇地询问我的口袋，我的表再一次安全了一段时间。之后，我想方设法找到了一件新的皮革，并将表放在里面，藏在了我的衬衣口袋里。无论我的身体或衣服有多么潮湿，这块表都始终完好无损并保持干燥。

持续了大概70天的分工劳作后，我们再一次回到死亡行军中，步行到了卡巴那端战俘集中营。我在这里待了两年半。我取下表的绷带，用药、纱布和胶带裹住表面，这样的包既小又易于藏匿。最终，我所在的集中营得到解放，我带着表回到家。进门后，我得知母亲已经去世了。如今，这块表让我回忆着自己的劫后重生，也让我回忆着母亲的一生。

我将表放回到它原来的盒子中，并加了一条与原来相同的链子。母亲的表再次成为一款精美的女士纪念表，我将它送给了妻子。后来，我发现我的兄弟还保留着原先的表链。当听说我要重修这块表时，他将表链送给了我。如今，在母亲买这块表的84年之后，我的女儿戴上了那块表。它还一直在工作着。

It was a seventeen-jewel Elgin in a locket-style case, and my mother bought it before she was married in September 1916. It was a typical watch of the era, functional yet decorative—a prized piece of jewelry for a woman of that time. When you pressed on the winding stem, the locket would spring open, exposing the face of the timepiece. The watch was given to me around the time I was thirteen or fourteen, and I had it converted into a wrist watch. For me, it was just another one of the things I owned. When I left for the service in April 1941, I took the watch with me.

My unit was sent to the Philippine Islands. On board ship, crossing the Pacific, I almost lost the watch after carelessly leaving it tied to a waterline while taking a shower. Thankfully, an honest GI found it and returned it. The watch still did not seem that special to me. It was just one of my practical possessions.

After the bombing of Pearl Harbor, we retreated to the Bataan Peninsula. Now I started to become a little concerned about my watch. With the enemy so close by, I felt foolish for bringing something that had been given to me by my mother. When we were told to surrender to the Japanese. I knew that my watch could become a Japanese souvenir. I couldn't bring myself to throw it into the jungle, but I didn't want to lose it to the enemy, either. I did what I could to outsmart my captors. I fastened the watch onto my left ankle and pulled my sock over it. For more protection, I put on a pair of leggings. Little did I know that I was about to embark on thirty-four months of playing a "hide the watch" game.

My unit surrendered, and then we were forced into the now infamous Bataan Death March. I wrapped the band around the watch and squeezed it into the small watch pocket of my pants. One day, while out on a work detail in northern Luzon, I was standing in the dump box of a truck, guarded by one of the ever present Japanese soldiers. His eyes were at just the right level to notice the lump in my small pocket. He reached out with a gloved hand and touched the spot. I froze and held my breath, fearing that I was about to lose my now prized possession. Surprisingly, the guard was not curious enough to ask about what I had in my pocket, and again the watch was safe for a while. Later, I managed to find a new chamois, and I swaddled the watch in it, concealing it in my shirt pocket. No matter how wet I became, the watch remained safe and dry.

The work detail lasted about seventy days. After that, it was back to another death march and on to Cabanatuan Prison Camp where I remained for two and a half years. There I removed the band from the watch and wrapped the face in medical gauze and tape. It made a small, easy-to-hide package. At last, when my camp was liberated, the watch and I made the trip home. When I walked through the door, I learned that my mother had died. Now her watch, which had become a reminder of my own survival, was also a reminder of her life.

I had the watch restored to its original case and added a chain identical to the original. Once again, my mother's watch was a delicate ladies' locket-style watch. I gave it to my wife. Later, I found that my brother still had the original watch chain. When he heard that I had restored the watch, he gave me the chain. Now, eighty-four years after my mother bought it, my daughter wears the watch. It is still in working condition.

母女之爱，
浩如烟海

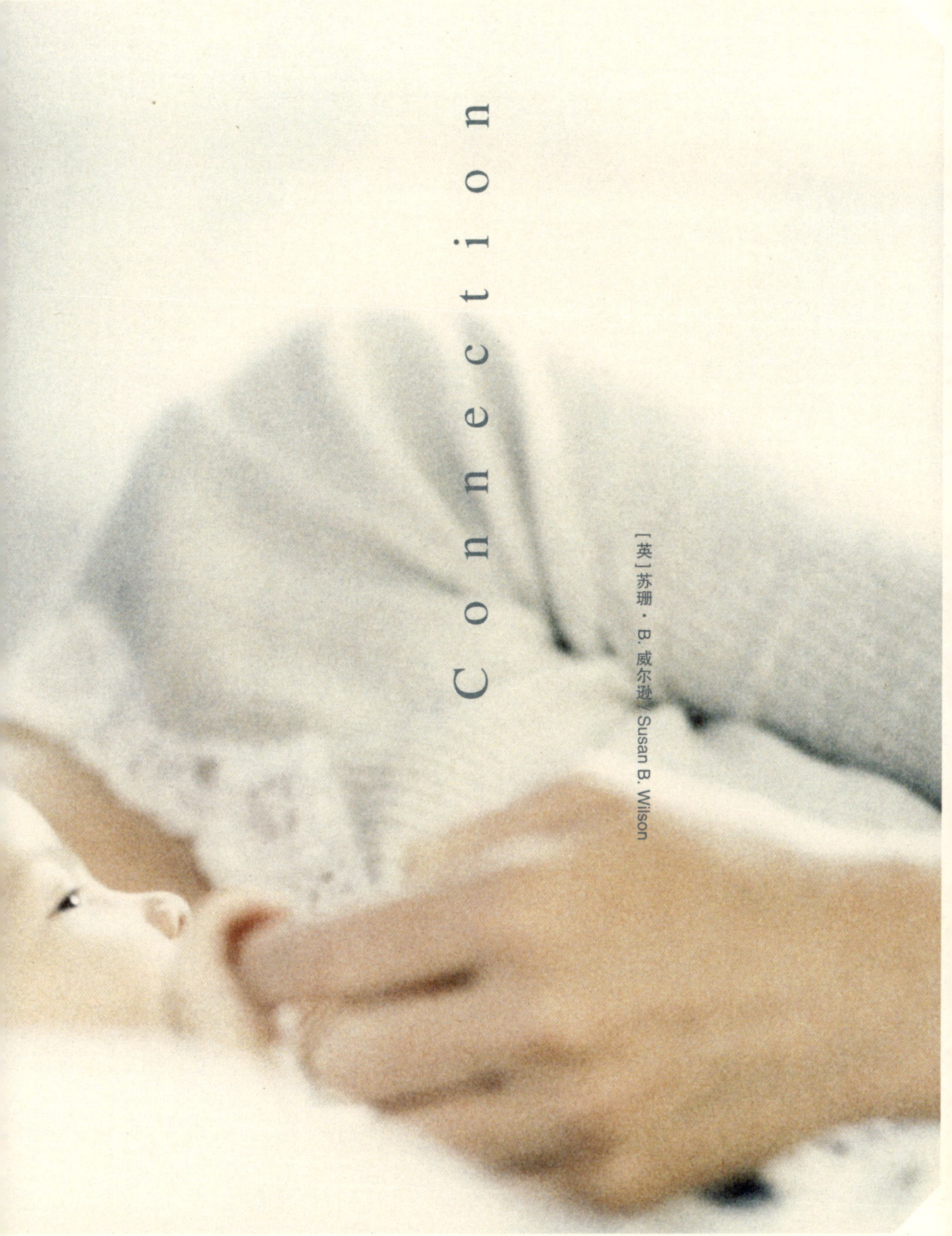

Connection

[英] 苏珊·B. 威尔逊 / Susan B. Wilson

因为我们所具有的非凡的默契和感知能力，我和母亲之间存在着深厚的母女情结。

14 年前，我住在印第安纳州的埃文斯维尔市，那里距离我的母亲——我的知己、我最好的朋友有八百英里。一天早上，沉思中的我突然觉得急需给母亲打个电话，问问她身体是否还好。起初，我犹豫了。因为母亲是四年级的老师，7：15打电话给她会打乱她的日常规律，使她上班迟到。但是，还是有某种力量驱使着我放下一切顾虑打给了她。我们聊了三分钟，她向我保证自己很安全、很健康。

那天晚些时候，我的电话铃声响起。是母亲打来的，她告诉我说，可能是我早上打给她的电话让她逃过了一劫。如果她早三分钟出门的话，她就很可能是州际公路上交通事故中的一名受害者。在那场事故中，数人死亡，多人受伤。

八年前，我发现我怀上了我的第一个孩子。预产期是 3 月 15 日。我对医生说，推算的这个预产期太提前了，孩子会推迟到 3 月 29 日至 4 月 3 日之间出生，因为母亲在那个时候刚好可以休春假。当然，我希望宝宝出生的时候母亲在我身边。医生仍然坚持说预产期是在 3 月中旬，而我只是笑笑。最后，里德在 3 月 30 日出生，母亲在 3 月 31 日到达了。

六年前，我又怀孕了。医生说预产期是在 3 月底。我说这次孩子会提前出生，你可以猜到，那是因为母亲所在的学校在 3 月初放假。医生和我都笑了。结果，布雷妮在 3 月 8 日出世。

两年半前，母亲正与癌症作斗争。一段时间后，她精疲力竭，失去了食欲和讲话的能力。陪她在北卡罗来纳州度过一个周末后，我不得不准备乘飞机返回美国的中西部地区。我跪在母亲床边，拉着她的手说："妈妈，如果我能赶回来，您愿意等我吗？"母亲一边睁大双眼，一边努力地点点头。

两天后，我接到继父打来的电话。母亲的生命危在旦夕，家庭中的所有成员都聚到了一起，向她作最后的告别。他们打开扬声器，以便我能听到那边的仪式。

在那个晚上，我远隔数千里，尽力用自己最有爱意的声音跟母亲说了再见。然而，第二天清晨，电话里传来的消息却是：母亲还活着，不过一直处于昏迷之中，随时都有可能辞世。可是她没有。不仅那天没有，第二天也没有。每天早上，我都能得到相同的电话消息：她随时都有可能撒手人寰，但是她没有。我的心痛和悲伤在每日里沉积。

漫长的数周过去了，我才终于明白：母亲是在等我。母亲曾向我表示，如果我能赶回来，她会等我。之前我不能赶回去，可是现在我能了。于是，我立即订购了机票。

到那天下午 5 点时，我已搂着母亲躺在她的床上了。母亲还在昏迷之中，但是我还是轻声对她说："妈妈，我在您身边了。您可以放心地走了。谢谢您等我，您可以放心地走了。"几个小时后，母亲离我们而去。

我想，当一种情结很深厚、很强大时，它会在言语无法表达的地方永存，它具有难以言表的美丽。尽管失去母亲带给我很深的伤痛，但母女情结的美丽和力量是任何东西都无法从我这里换取的。

My mother and I are deeply connected by our uncanny ability to silently communicate with each other.

Fourteen years ago, I was living in Evansville, Indiana, 800 miles away from my mother—my confidante, my best friend. One morning, while in a quiet state of contemplation, I suddenly felt an urgent need to call Mother and ask if she was all right. At first I hesitated. Since my mother taught fourth grade, calling her at 7:15 A.M. could interrupt her routine and made her late for work. But something compelled me to go ahead and call her. We spoke for three minutes, and she assured me that she was safe and fine.

Later that day, the telephone rang. It was Mother, reporting that my morning phone call had probably saved her life. Had she left the house three minutes earlier, it's likely that she would have been part of a major interstate accident that killed several people and injured many more.

Eight years ago, I discovered that I was pregnant with my first child. The due date was March 15th. I told the doctor that was just too soon. The baby's due date had to fall between March 29th and April 3th because that was when my mother had her spring break from teaching. And of course I wanted her with me. The doctor still insisted that the due date was mid-March. I just smiled. Reid arrived on March 30. Mother arrived on March 31th.

Six years ago, I was expecting again. The doctor said the due date was toward the end of March. I said it would have to be earlier this time because—you guessed it—Mother's school break was near the beginning of March. The doctor and I both smiled. Breanne made her entry on March 8th.

Two and a half years ago, Mother was fighting cancer. Over time, she lost her energy, her appetite, her ability to speak. After a weekend with her in North Carolina, I had to prepare for my flight back to the Midwest. I knelt at Mother's bedside and took her hand. "Mother, if I can, do you want me to come back?" Her eyes widened as she tried to nod.

Two days later, I had a call from my stepfather. My mother was dying. Family members were gathered for last rites. They put me on a speakerphone to hear the service.

That night, I tried my best to send a loving goodbye to Mother over the miles. The next morning, however, the telephone rang: Mother was still alive, but in a coma and expected to die any minute. But she didn't. Not that day, or the next. Every morning, I'd get the same call: She could die any minute. But she didn't. And every day, my pain and sadness were compounded.

After long weeks passed, it finally dawned on me: Mother was waiting for me. She had communicated that she wanted me to come back if I could. I hadn't been able to before, but now I could. I made reservation immediately.

By 5:00 that afternoon, I was lying in her bed with my arms around her. She was still in a coma, but I whispered, "I'm here, Mother. You can let go. Thank you for waiting. You can let go." She died just a few hours later.

I think when a connection is that deep and powerful, it lives forever in a place far beyond words and is indescribably beautiful. For all the agony of my loss, I would not trade the beauty and power of that connection for anything.

田间之旅
Field Trip

［美］伊万·盖尔福德—布雷克
Evan Guilfore-Blake

我读的第一所学校坐落在一座小荒山的山顶，校舍是一间平房，屋顶上插了一个风向标。校舍的周围是农田（农田里还有一个牲畜棚，用来养家畜），当时那片地方还不属于伊利诺伊州的乌尔班纳。回想起来，那所学校有6个班级，共有35名学生，大部分是一些年龄较小的孩子，当然也有十二三岁的。

1953年，父亲在伊利诺伊大学读哲学博士，6岁的我在上一年级。我的同学和高年级学生中的大部分都是农民出身的孩子，有的是享受《美国退伍军人法案》福利的士兵大学生的子女，有的是因为家里太穷无法在城市生活并享受那里的教育。至于我，早期教育主要是父母在家给予的，不会有太大的影响。

学校里只有一名教师——柯耐普夫人。柯耐普夫人是一名职业教师，她与学校的建筑物看起来一样古老。柯耐普夫人说，她从事了一辈子教育工作，我猜想，她那时应该已经做了35~40年的教育工作了。柯耐普夫人的头发已经全白了，但梳理得很整齐，我想她大概已经六十多岁了。

柯耐普夫人在教学上因材施教，而且对于这种方法已经很有经验了。对于已经能够欣赏史蒂文森和鲍勃先生的诗歌的学生，还有那些读《狄克和珍妮的故事》有些困难的学生，她都能进行指导。假如把一个年级看成是一个不同的国家，那么柯耐普夫人就是一个能流利地讲六种语言的人。不论是学习上，还是在其他方面，柯耐普夫人总能找到适当而又令人好奇的话题。比如说，她所知道的棒球和棒球历史的知识就要比我的父亲多得多，而且总是很乐意与你讨论棒球游击手皮·维·雷斯相对于奇科·卡拉斯科尔的优点，其中雷斯是她最喜欢的选手，而卡拉斯科尔是我最喜欢的选手。

柯耐普夫人在我的记忆中留下了一件终身难忘的事情，然而，这件事情不是发生在学校里，而是在乡村玉米田间的一条小路上。第一学年结束的那天下午，天气非常好，她带着我们去田野游玩，准确地说，那是一片种着玉米和小麦的农田，这些庄稼长得比我们还高，也比柯耐普夫人高。绿色的玉米和小麦秆已经变黄，但是还需要两三个月才能收割。

我们漫步于田间，柯耐普夫人耐心地给我们讲述着田间的每一只虫子、每一只小鸟以及每一

片树叶。我们像大多数孩子一样，眼睛入迷地捕捉着她给我们讲述的一切。我们沿着那条铺着沙砾的土路走着，这是一条不通车的路，道路的宽度仅够一辆拖拉机或一辆小汽车通过，一路上看不到一棵树。伊利诺伊草原地势平坦，但我们只能看到地平线上蓝色的天空，偶尔也能看到庄稼地尽头露出的农舍屋顶。我们停下来，在路边吃午餐——三明治，耳边传来风吹过庄稼发出的沙沙声，还有乌鸦、蟋蟀和甲虫发出的叫声，眼前是随风摇摆的庄稼。

我们在吃过午餐后继续向前走，然而眼前只是一片又一片的庄稼，耳边是一阵又一阵的鸟叫声，就像是重复前面的旅行，我和其他人一样，开始失去耐心。就在那时，奇迹出现了，在几百码外的另一条田间小路的一侧，坐落着一家冰淇淋店（几年以后，我想起来就感觉那是从《城市贫民区》或者史蒂芬·金的小说里突然冒出来的一样）。这家小店只

是一个 6~8 英尺长、2 英尺宽、5 英尺高的木柜台，柜台上醒目地印着"冰淇淋——10种口味"，柜台上是一个由几根杆子支起来的遮阳用的木板。一个头发斑白的中年男子面带笑容地站在柜台后面。

柯耐普夫人与这名男子互相打了招呼，就像老朋友一样。然后，她转身对我们说，她请客，每个人要一个任何口味的冰淇淋。大家一下子变得兴高采烈。曾经吃过的巧克力和香草口味的冰淇淋，味道不错，大家商量着是要吃过的，还是尝尝外来的罗克杰或蓝莓冰淇淋。最后，每个人挑选了自己想吃的口味，那个中年男人给我们每人都挖了一大勺。大家一边享受着冰淇淋的香味，一边大口地吃起来。

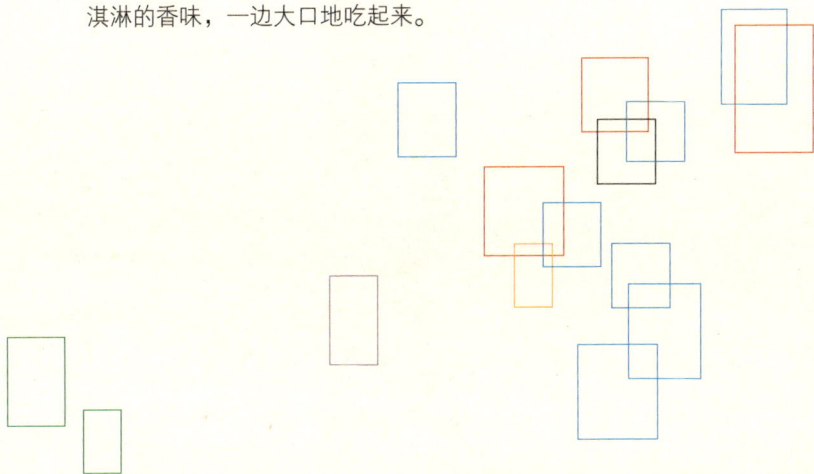

然后，那个男人问柯耐普夫人："您想要什么口味的？"我记得，他说话的时候眼睛眨了一下，随后两个人就客套起来。即使几年前与柯耐普夫人来过这个地方的那些学生，也不知道这个冰淇淋店。

柯耐普夫人想了一下，说："每个口味来一勺，都装在一个盒子里吧。"

我们都惊讶地睁大眼睛，然而那个男人眼睛眨也没眨。一样一勺？10种口味？装在一个盒子里？柯耐普夫人比年龄最大的学生还要瘦弱，她居然能吃10勺冰淇淋！

她从那个男人的手里小心翼翼地接过冰淇淋后，舔了舔冰淇淋的顶部，并发出了"啧啧"的赞美声，表情就像给我们上课时那样沉着。我们站在那里羡慕地看着，她的舌头舔着冰淇淋的每一部分，从草莓味的转到核桃味的，不让夏日的炎热带走一滴。

50 年后的今天，我已经记不清第一个学年的事情了，唯有柯耐普夫人和 10 勺超级装冰淇淋深深地留在了记忆中。现代的大冰淇淋店卖的冰淇淋有 20~30 种口味，当我看到孩子们坐在冰淇淋店外面时，就会想到，柯耐普夫人是不是手里拿着一个装满冰淇淋的华夫蛋卷，一边注视着这些孩子，一边高兴地品尝呢？

然后，我们走了大约一英里就回到了学校。大家整理好各自的东西，相互告别后，就走回家或等待父母来接。

我当然会把这件事讲给父母听，他们自然笑了。放暑假后的第二周，我们开车经过学校，柯耐普夫人离开了，学校的大门也已经关上了。我当时就想，柯耐普夫人和她的丈夫一定吃过很多冰淇淋，而那些冰淇淋应该是装在超级包装盒里的。后来，我们就再也没有见到过柯耐普夫人，我们去找了那个冰淇淋店，可是也没有找到。

My first school was the storied one-room schoolhouse. An old white washed building with a red roof and a vane on the peak, it sat at the top of an unpaved hill surrounded by farmland.including a barn rife with livestock.in a then-unincorporated area of Urbana, Ilinois. The school housed all six primary grades and, as I recall, there were about thirty-five of us, mostly very young, although we ranged in age, of course, up to twelve or thirteen.

The year was 1953, and I was six years old, a first grader, and the son of a Ph. D. student at the University of Ilinois. My peers and the upper graders were farm kids or children of undergrads taking advantage of the GI Bill. Some were just too poor to live in the city, which would have qualified them for a city school. I suspect my parents dismissed the relevance of first grade, since most of my education came at home, at their hands, anyway.

The sole teacher in that school was as classic as the building itself. Mrs. Knapp was a schoolmarm by profession and she'd been doing it, she said, all her life. By then, I'd guess, that meant thirty-five or forty years on the job. She had to have been in her sixties: white hair in perfect array.

She handled our diverse intellects with perfect aplomb, guiding those of us who could read well through the pleasures of Stevenson's poetry and Mr. Popper and those who struggled with reading through the joys of Dick and Jane. If every grade was a different country, Mrs. Knapp was fluent in the six languages we spoke, always having appropriate conversation to offer on whatever subject— academic and not—that our curiosity was heir to. She knew, for example, more about baseball and its history than my father did and was always ready to argue the merits of Pee Wee Reese (her favorite shortstop) against Chico Carrasquel (mine).

The one Mrs. Knapp incident that will always remain engraved in my memory didn't happen at school, however. It happened on a deserted country road that divided corn-fields on the afternoon of the last day of that, my first full-fledged school year. To celebrate the beautiful weather, she'd taken us on a field trip, literally, through the bright yellow and green of corn and wheat stalks that were taller than I was （and than she was, too） but still two or three months shy of their harvest.

We wandered, as large groups of children are wont to do, our eyes catching with fascination on every bug and bird and leaf, every one of which, unfailingly, Mrs. Knapp had explanations for. We trekked along utterly untrafficked gravel and dirt roads that had been bulldozed just wide enough for tractors or a single car to travel. There were no trees: The Ilinois prairie land was flat, and we could see only the blue of the horizon and an occasional farmhouse rooftop beyond the fields of grain. We ate our lunch sandwiches along a roadside, listening to the rustle of the wind through the gently waving crops, the cries of the crows, the chirrs of the crickets and beetles.

After lunch we walked more. Now, though, the trip had become repetitious—more fields, more crops, more birdcalls—and I, certainly among others, was becoming impatient. Then, it happened: There, in the absolute middle of nowhere （straight out of what, some years later, I would think of as The Twilight Zone or a Stephen King novel）, on the side of another single-lane road hundreds of yards from anything that resembled civilization, stood an ice cream stand. Nothing fancy, just a wooden counter six or eight feet wide, five feet high, two feet deep, with poles supporting a wood sheet that served as sun cover for the grizzled, but smiling, middle-aged man who stood behind it. The words "Ice Cream—10 Flavors" were painted prominently on the front.

The man and Mrs. Knapp greeted each other as old friends. She turned to us and said each of us could have an ice cream cone, any flavor we wished, her treat. Our enthusiasm was, naturally, boundless, and debate over whether to stick to the known delights of chocolate or vanilla or whether to experiment with the exotic Rocky Road or Blueberry raged among us. But we each settled on something, and the man scooped large scoops into waffle cones and handed them out. We savored and devoured.

Then he asked Mrs. Knapp, " What would you like? " I like to think there was a twinkle in his eyes as he did and that what followed was a ritual between them, although the few kids who'd attended Mrs. Knapp's classes in years before hadn't been to the stand.

She paused thoughtfully, then said, " I think I'll have a cone with a scoop of each."

He didn't bat an eyelash, but we did. A scoop of each? All ten flavors? In one cone? Mrs. Knapp, this woman who was smaller than the oldest of her students, was going to eat a ten-scoop ice cream cone?

With the same aplomb she displayed in the classroom, she took the mountain from him carefully and licked the top. She said something like " Mmm" and smiled. And we watched, agog with envy, as she consumed every sweet mound, moving her tongue up and down from vanilla to strawberry to butter pecan, not losing a drop to the heat of the afternoon.

Afterward, we walked back to the school, perhaps just a mile or so away, packed up our things, said good-bye to her and each other, and walked home or waited for our parents to come.

Of course, I told my parents about the event, and, of course, they smiled. We drove past the school the following week. It was closed for the summer and Mrs. Knapp was off somewhere, with Mr. Knapp, I supposed, eating copious quantities of ice cream stacked in sky-high cones. I never saw her again, and though we looked, I never found that ice cream stand, either.

Now, fifty years later, though the little else I can recall about that first school year is only dimly remembered, Mrs. Knapp and her ten-scoop ice cream cone remains one of my clearest childhood memories. And often, as I watch children sitting in the sun outside modern twenty-or thirty-flavor ice cream emporiums, I wonder if perhaps she isn't somewhere watching, a well-filled waffle cone in hand, still enjoying it mightily.

妈妈，我爱你

Tell Mommy I Love Her

佚名 / Anonymous

三个多星期以来，约翰一直忙得不可开交，不停地联系客户。他情不自禁地想回俄亥俄州去看看妻子和孩子们。母亲节到了，以往的母亲节他都会尽可能回家，但今年他太疲倦了。在小石城外的一个小镇上，他途经一家花店。他对自己说："我知道该怎么做了，我会给妈妈寄些玫瑰花。"

他来到这家花店，看到一个男孩正在跟店员说话。"小姐，请问6美元可以买多少玫瑰花？"男孩问道。店员尽力说明玫瑰花很昂贵，或许康乃馨会符合他的意愿。

"不，我必须要玫瑰花。"他说，"我妈妈去年生病时，十分虚弱，而我没有花很多时间和她在一起。我想送她一些特别的东西。那一定是玫瑰花，因为妈妈最喜爱玫瑰。"他的态度很坚决。

店员抬头看着约翰，只是不住地摇头。约翰内心深处被男孩的话语触动了，男孩是多么迫切地想要得到那些玫瑰花。约翰的生意一直不错。于是他看了看店员，然后小声对她说自己愿意为男孩买玫瑰花。

店员看了看男孩，说道："好吧，我收你 6 美元，给你一打玫瑰花。"男孩高兴地差点儿要跳起来。他接过花，然后跑出了花店。看到小男孩如此兴奋，约翰觉得这额外的 35 美元没有白花。

约翰订购了自己要的花，一再叮嘱店员确认给母亲的花中要附上一张便条，写上他有多爱她。开车离开花店时，他的心情出奇的好。因为红灯，他在离花店约两个街区的地方停了下来。就在等红灯的过程中，他看见那个男孩正走过人行道。约翰目送男孩穿过大街，经过两扇巨大的门进入了一个公园。突然，他意识到那不是公园，而是一块墓地。他还能看到男孩在大门那儿转过身，沿着篱笆向前走去。

M

o

m

m

y

绿灯亮了，约翰慢慢地把车开过十字路口，停在路边。他一冲动下了车，开始沿着篱笆跟着男孩。那个男孩来到了篱笆围着的墓地，约翰与他保持着三四十步的距离，在人行道上跟着他。男孩在一块小小的墓碑前止住脚步，然后跪了下来。他小心翼翼地将花放在坟上，然后开始哭泣。约翰觉得自己是一个入侵者，但他又不忍离开。他看着男孩因哭泣而上下起伏的身体，听着他低低的哭声。

男孩夹杂着哭泣的话语传到约翰的耳朵里：

"妈妈，哦，妈妈，为什么我没告诉你我有多爱你？为什么我没有再一次告诉你？上帝，求你找到我妈妈，告诉她我爱她！"

约翰泪流满面地转过身来，走回自己的车里。他飞快地开着车回到那家花店，告诉店员他要亲手把花交给妈妈。他想要亲自把花送给妈妈，并再一次告诉她，他有多爱她。

John had been on the road visiting clients for more than three weeks. He couldn't wait to get back to Ohio to see his wife and children. It was coming up on Mother's Day, and he usually tried to make it "back home", but this year he was just too tired. He was in a small town just outside of Little Rock when he drove by a flower shop. He said to himself, "I know what I will do, I'll send Mom some roses."

He went into the small shop and saw a young man talking to the clerk. "How many roses can I get for six dollars, ma'am? " the boy asked. The clerk was trying to explain that roses were expensive.

Maybe the young man would be happy with carnations. "No. I have to have roses," he said, "My Mom was sick so much last year and I didn't get to spend much time with her. I want to get something special. It has to be red roses, because that's her favorite." He was emphatic.

The clerk looked up at John and was just shaking her head. Something inside of John was touched by the boy's voice. He wanted to get those roses so bad. John had been blessed in his business, and he looked at the clerk and silently mouthed that he would pay for the boy's roses.

The clerk looked at the young man and said, "Okay, I will give you a dozen red roses for your six dollars."The young man almost jumped into the air. He took the flowers and ran from the store. It was worth the extra thirty-five dollars just to see that kind of excitement.

John ordered his own flowers and had the clerk be sure that delivery would include a note telling his mother how much he loved her. As he drove away from the shop, he was feeling very good. He caught a light about two blocks from the shop. As he waited at the light, he saw the young boy walking down the sidewalk. He watched him cross the street and enter a park through two huge gates. Suddenly, he realized it wasn't a park. It was a cemetery. He could see the young man turn there by gate and walk along the fence.

The light changed, and John slowly crossed the intersection. He pulled over and on an impulse got out and began to follow the boy down the fence line. John was on the sidewalk, thirty or forty steps behind the boy, who walked inside the cemetery fence. The young man stopped by a small monument and went on his knees. He carefully laid the roses on the grave and began to sob. John felt like an intruder but he couldn't leave. He stared at the little boy's heaving body and listened to his muted crying.

As he cried, he heard the young man speak, "Mommy, oh Mommy, why didn't I tell you how much I love you. Why didn't I tell you one more time? Jesus, please, find my Mommy. Tell my Mommy I love her."

John turned, tears in his eyes, and walked back to his car. He drove quickly to the florist and told her he would take the flowers personally. He wanted to be sure and tell his Mother one more time just how much he loved her.

鸽子的

Abigal's Dove

奇迹

〔美〕卡伦·马约里·加里森/Karen Majoris Garrison

这是十年里最大的一场暴风雪，我被困在其中。提前听说了晚上可能会下雪的消息，我便自愿到教堂去帮助发放一些食物和药品给那些有需要的老人。因为丈夫出差了，于是我打电话给母亲，让她来照看我三岁大的女儿阿比盖尔。母亲很快就过来了。

母亲担心我的安危，问道："难道别人不能帮助他们吗？我有一种不好的预感，似乎大雪随时都会下起来。"

我瞥了一眼窗外，不得不承认，天空正变得越来越阴沉。我也开始感觉不踏实了。

"妈妈不会有事的。"正牵着外婆的手的女儿笑着说道，"因为她乐于助人。而且，我会为妈妈祈祷的！"

女儿的话让我的心绪澎湃起来。我们的关系是如此亲密，以至于有时候我们会心有灵犀。于是，我决定去践行对女儿的教导：有时我们需要真实地迈出自己的脚步，并且相信上帝一定会保佑我们的。与母亲和女儿吻别之后，我出发去挨家挨户地给老人们送东西。当我送到最后一家时，天空开始下起雪来。

92 岁的比尔·瓦肯是我们教会中的一名成员，他责骂道："你不应该来这里的。"比尔·瓦肯挣扎着想要从床上下来，可是他咳嗽得很厉害，有些力不从心。他只好放弃，又躺回到枕头上说："我告诉过牧师，不希望今天有人来这么偏远的郊区看我。"

"别胡说了。"我一边笑着说，一边将食物和饮料放在他的床边。尽管比尔外表粗鲁，可是有一颗美好的心灵。他每天都需要服用治疗心脏的药物，他没有家人，仅靠着微薄的收入度日，他需要尽可能多的帮助。

"哎，看你任性的结果是什么。"他指着窗外积雪覆盖的道路对我说，"留在这儿吧，卡伦，我希望你是安全的。"

我吻了一下他的头顶，决定勇敢地面对糟糕的路况。我的理由是，再不走情况会更糟。

想着我可爱的女儿在我临走之前所说的话，我对比尔·瓦肯说："我不会有事的。"想起阿比盖尔，更让我坚定了回家的信心。我已经想念我的女儿了。

钻进车里，我努力使车沿着陡峭的山路逐渐向下行驶。心里想着雪中驾车规则，我保持着二挡的行驶速度。风力加强了，雪也随风扬起，挡住了我的视线。我一边斜视着挡风玻璃，一边屏住呼吸小心驾驶着。我尖叫着转动方向盘，差一点儿撞上那只站在我车灯前的冻僵的麋鹿。

我的车撞在路堤上，从路边垂直落下，掉入底部的一个峡谷。当车子最终停止了旋转时，我睁开眼睛，意识到有一段时间我失去了意识。夜晚来了——预报中的大雪也来了。惊恐万分的我试图打开车门，可是车门被积雪堵住，怎么也推不动。我爬到旁边的副驾驶座位上，发现那扇门被一棵树卡住了。我转动钥匙想要启动引擎，可是电池没电了。因此，摇下车窗爬出车外的希望也落空了。没有暖气和足够的衣物保暖，我蜷缩在后座上等待救助。

寒冷的空气笼罩了我。我颤抖着，责怪自己没作好应对这样的环境的准备。我的脚趾和手指已冻得麻木。似乎很久过后，当我听到风与雪交织着抽打车子的声音时，我开始为此刻正在为我担忧的家人祈祷。我回到家的时候，阿比盖尔也许为我画画了。自从她可以握住画笔之后，她就为她所爱之人做画，来使他们的生活变得明亮。

我更加担心自己的安危，为了让这种愈加强烈的担忧平静下来，我闭上双眼，让自己集中精力回想那些高兴的事情。渐渐地，我睡着了，梦里看到了阿比盖尔。她站在温暖的阳光里，笑着递给我一只美丽的白鸽。白鸽的优雅安静，还有女儿眼中闪烁的爱意，让我觉得很安详。

晚上，天气变得更加寒冷，当我的意识时而清醒，时而模糊时，我将自己的思绪集中在想象阿比盖尔和她的白鸽上。它们陪伴我度过了整个漫长的夜晚。数小时后，当黎明的第一束光亮出现时，我听到有人在拍打我的车窗。我放心地看到有一支急救队。就在他们把我抬到担架上面，送进救护车时，我那僵硬的嘴唇露出了一丝微笑。在医院里，医生诊断我为轻度冻伤，头部的一个伤口需要住院观察一晚才有结果。我急切地想见到家人，靠着枕头坐在病床上，焦急地等待着家人的出现。

没多久，病房的门开了，母亲冲了进来。她猛地抱住我，哭着说道："我们快担心死了！我就知道你遇上麻烦了！母亲就是能预感到。"当她评价旁边的餐盘时，她的母性便表现了出来。她说："你的茶凉了！我去去就来。"

阿比盖尔抓住只有我们两个人的机会，爬上床，将脸埋在我的脖子里。我把她抱得更近些，用手将她那丝滑的头发从脸上拂开，轻声对她说："我好想你。我离开的时间里，你都做了些什么？"

"噢，我都忘记了！"她兴奋地叫道，并挣脱了我的怀抱，抓起旁边的一卷纸张。"昨晚不知道你在哪里的时候，我为你画了这张画。我想你可能会感到害怕，我希望你能感觉好点。"

就好像这是一张藏宝图一样，我打开它，惊讶于眼前看到的画面。我指着上面红色的方块说："噢，那是我们的车子。"我用指尖指着一个有长头发的棒状小人，笑着说："那个是我。可是，我手中拿的是什么？"

当她将指尖落在画面上那个小物体时，阿比盖尔的眼睛明亮起来。她兴奋地说道："是上帝的灵魂。我把它画成了鸽子，就像我在主日学校里看到的那样。"她用那柔软的嘴唇在我的脸颊上吻了一下，然后补充说："妈妈，我不想让你孤单，于是我就画了我能想到的最好的朋友给你。"

回想起在那个最黑暗的夜晚带给我安慰的白鸽，我惊呼起来："天哪，亲爱的，你的鸽子真的陪伴在我身边。"我握着她的手，为母女之间的心有灵犀感到震惊。

"你们在看什么？"母亲打断了我们，将一杯热气腾腾的茶放在床头的茶几上。她转身准备走开，而我却抓住她的手，放在我和阿比盖尔的手指间。三代人之间的这种奇妙的关联，给我们一种极其特别的感觉。

"我们正在看我们之间的爱流。"我轻声说道。亲吻女儿的头顶时，我的目光与母亲会心的目光相遇。我再次凝视着阿比盖尔的画，仔细看着出现在如此恐怖的夜晚的这只鸟儿，它将我与女儿的心紧紧连接在一起。

很多年后，我们母女间那个特别的夜晚，成为我们熟知的"奇迹"。那是阿比盖尔的鸽子的奇迹。

It bad been the worst snowstorm in ten years, and I'd been caught in it. After hearing earlier that it was supposed to snow later in the night, I had volunteered at our church to take groceries and medical prescriptions to elderly members in need. Since my husband was away on business, I called my mother and she immediately came over to my house to watch my three-year-old daughter, Abigail.

"Can't someone else help those people? " she had asked me, concerned for my safety. "I have a bad feeling about this, and it looks like it might snow at any minute."

I glanced out the window and had to admit that the sky looked threatening. I began to feel uncertain.

"Mama will be okay," my daughter smiled, taking her grandmother's hand, "She likes helping people. Besides, I'll be praying for her!"

My heart swelled at her words. We had such a close relationship that sometimes when I breathed, it was as though Abigail exhaled. I decided then that I had to act on what I'd been instilling in my daughter: that sometimes we just have to step out in faith and believe that God will keep us safe. Kissing my mother and daughter good-bye, I set out to make my rounds. On my last stop, the snow began to fall.

"You shouldn't have come here." Bill Watkins, a ninety-two-year-old member of our congregation, scolded. He coughed, trying to get out of bed, but the effort proved too taxing. Giving up, he settled back on to the pillows. "I told the pastor that I didn't expect anyone to come to the boonies for me."

"Nonsense." I grinned, positioning snacks and drinks by his bed. Beneath his gruff exterior, Bill was sweet as candy. His heart medication had to be taken every day, and living on a modest income without any surviving family members, he needed as much help as possible.

"Well, look what your stubbornness brought you." he said, pointing to the snow-covered road outside the window. His fingers clasped my hand. "Stay here, Karen. I want you safe."

I kissed the top of his head but decided to brave the road conditions. It would be worse later, I reasoned.

"I'll be okay." I told him, remembering my sweet daughter's words before I left. Thoughts of Abigail made me more determined to get home. I missed her already.

I got into my Volkswagen and gradually tried making it down the steep hill. Remembering old instructions about driving in the snow, I kept the compact car in second gear. The wind increased, creating waves of blinding white. As I squinted through the windshield, holding my breath, I screamed and jerked the wheel, narrowly missing the deer that stood frozen by my headlights.

The Volkswagen hit the embankment, plummeted off the side of the road, and skidded to the bottom of a ravine below. When the rolling motion finally stopped, I opened my eyes and realized that I had been unconscious for some time. Night had arrived—and with it the forecasted accumulation of snow. Panicking, I tried opening the door, but it wouldn't budge against the resisting snow. Sliding over to the passenger's door, I realized that the door had been jammed shut by a tree. I turned the key to start the engine, but the battery was dead. My hopes of rolling down the power windows to crawl out vanished. Without heat and adequate clothing, I curled up on the back seat and waited for help.

The frigid air enveloped me. Shivering, I chastised myself for not preparing for a circumstance like this. My toes and fingers were already numb. An eternity seemed to pass, and as I listened to the wind and snow hitting against the car, I prayed for my family, who would be sick with worry by now. Abigail would probably be drawing pictures for me when I arrived home. Since she'd been old enough to hold a crayon, she'd drawn pictures to brighten the days of her loved ones.

To calm my growing concern about my safety, I closed my eyes and concentrated on pleasant thoughts. Drifting into sleep, I saw Abigail. Abigail in the warm sunlight, laughing as she held out a beautiful white dove to me. The dove's graceful, serene presence and the love shining in my daughter's eyes filled me with peace.

The night grew colder, and as I floated in and out of consciousness, I fixed my mind on the image of Abigail and her dove. Together, they kept me company throughout the night. Hours later, as the first rays of daybreak appeared, I heard tapping on my window. Relieved to see an emergency rescue team, my stiff lips tried to smile as they hoisted me onto a stretcher and into an ambulance. At the hospital, I was treated for mild frostbite and a head wound before being told I'd have to stay overnight for observation. Anxious to see my family, I propped myself up on the bed pillows and waited impatiently.

Before long, the door opened and my mother burst into the room. "We were so worried about you!" she cried, rushing over to hug me. "I knew you were in trouble!Mothers sense these kinds of things." Her maternal instincts surfaced as she appraised the food tray nearby. "Your tea is cold! I'll be right back."

Seizing the opportunity to have me all to herself, Abigail climbed onto the bed and buried her face in my neck. I scooped her closer. "I've missed you so much." I murmured softly, brushing a silky strand of hair from her face. "And what have you been doing while I've been away? "

"Oh, I forgot!" she exclaimed, jumping out of my arms to grab a large tube of construction paper nearby. "I drew this for you last night when we didn't know where you were. I thought you might have been scared, and I wanted you to feel better."

As if it were a treasure map, I unrolled it and oohed and aahed over the images. "Well, that's our car." I said, pointing to the red square. "And that's me." I laughed, touching my fingertips to a stick person with long hair. "But what am I holding? "

Abigail's eyes brightened as she pushed her fingertip to the small object on the paper. "That's God's spirit." she said excitedly. "I drew it as a dove like I saw in Sunday school." She pressed her soft lips against my cheek and added, "I didn't want you to be alone, Mama, and so I gave you the best friend I could think of."

"Oh, darling, " I exclaimed, recalling the white dove that had given me comfort in the darkest of nights. "Your dove was with me." Taking her hand, I marveled at the heavenly bond between mothers and daughters.

"And what are you two looking at? " my mother interrupted, placing a steaming cup of tea on the nightstand. She started to move away, but I grabbed her hand and brought it between Abigail's and mine. It was a remarkable feeling, this incredible connection of three generations.

"We're looking at the love that flows between us." I whispered, kissing the top of my daughter's head as I met my mother's understanding eyes. Returning my gaze to Abigail's picture, I studied the beautiful bird that had, on such a dismal night, connected my daughter's heart with mine.

Years later, that extraordinary event in our mother-daughter relationship became known as the "miracle". The miracle of Abigail's dove.

我最思念的人

My Most Unforgettable Charater

佚名 / Anonymous

妈妈的脸上洋溢着骄傲的光芒。我知道，我们所取得的和将要取得的每一点成就，都是我们的父母所赐。

在我们还是小孩子的时候，妈妈便是我们的良师益友。直到我长大成人，才意识到她是多么不平凡。

甘于奉献。母亲是在意大利北部的一个小镇出生的。1926年，她的父母移民到这个国家的时候，她才3岁。他们一家居住在芝加哥南区，在那里，我的外祖父做着冰淇淋生意。

在这个喧嚣的都市氛围中，妈妈茁壮成长着。16岁的时候，她以第一名的成绩从高中毕业，进入到文秘学校学习，并最终在铁路公司做行政秘书工作。

妈妈长得也很漂亮。当地的一位摄影师用她的照片作每月的橱窗展示，这令妈妈的心里美滋滋的。她最喜欢那张坐在密歇根湖畔的照片，照片上她眺望着远方，头发被风吹拂着。妈妈常说，一个人死去的时候，上帝就会将"最完美的自我"归还给他。她喜欢拿这张照片给我们看，她说："这就是我在天堂的样子。"

妈妈在1944年与父亲结了婚。父亲虽然少言寡语，却是一个很聪明的人。他17岁便离开了意大利。之后不久，他遭遇了一场肇事司机逃逸的交通事故，而这次事故让他永远成为了跛脚。父亲在芝加哥办公大楼里的工作人员休息的时候，向他们兜售糖果，他很勤奋地工作着。父亲没受过什么正规的教育，他的英语都是自学的。然而，他终于有了一家自己的小店，成功地做着糖果批发生意。爸爸不仅慷慨大方、相貌堂堂，还是一个虔诚的教徒。妈妈深深地爱上了他。

结婚后，妈妈辞去工作，做起了家庭主妇。1950 年，父亲带着母亲和 3 个孩子搬到一片农场居住，那里距离芝加哥有 40 英里。他既要做农田里的活，还要去城里做生意。妈妈离开她的父母和朋友，告别身边喧嚣的城市，过起了离群索居的生活。然而，母亲从来没有抱怨过。到了 1958 年，我们这座简朴的农舍里有了 6 个孩子，母亲很高兴。

胸怀大志。妈妈从来没有看过育儿方面的书籍，但她知道该如何养育她的孩子们。她提升我们的自尊心，帮助我们发挥自己的潜能。

秋日里的一天，我坐在餐桌前，妈妈正削着土豆皮。她透过窗子看到爸爸坐在拖拉机上，笑了，她自豪地说："你爸爸取得了这么多的成就，他真是个了不起的人！"

妈妈希望我们每个人也都能成为了不起的人。她总是说："你们的挑战就是做你能做之事，而我的挑战则是帮助你们去完成它们。"

她每天都会读书给我们听，还用自制的卡片教我们学语音。对于我们取得的最普通的小成就，母亲也会进行表扬，以此来增强我们的信心。10岁的时候，我把一对木板涂成白色，把它们钉在一起制成了一个不牢固的书架。"太棒了！"妈妈称赞道，"我们正需要一个书架呢！"这个摇摇晃晃的书架母亲一用就是很多年。

我家的餐厅里挂着两张按数字涂颜色的画，那是姐姐格罗丽亚和哥哥利欧小时候画的。几年前，利欧说那两幅画不是很好看，提议把它们取下来，母亲没有同意。她说："它们挂在那里是要提醒你们，孩提时的你们也是那么能干。"

从一开始，母亲就要求我们要胸怀大志。一天，在看望过居住在南区的外祖父母之后，母亲让父亲绕路而行，带着我们经过普鲁登希尔大厦的施工场地。母亲为我们解释说，工程竣工后，这座 41 层的大楼将成为芝加哥最高的建筑物。"或许有一天，你们当中的谁也能设计出这样的建筑物。"

母亲对我们的信心深深地感染了我们。12 岁的姐姐卡拉宣称，她将来要成为一名律师。

"你一定能的。世上无难事，只怕有心人。"妈妈对她说。

人生向导。对于妈妈而言，教育是她成功蓝图的一个重要部分。我们四兄妹去了附近只有一间教室的学校上学。通过为我们找来一些有教育意义的玩具，同我们一起探讨历史、政治和时事，帮助我们做好作业，母亲为我们弥补了学校教学的不足之处。取得优异成绩后，她对我们的赞扬是最好的事情。

当我读到三年级的时候，母亲劝说我们的老师组织一次芝加哥博物馆的实地参观。她还帮老师租借了汽车，安排了行程。母亲甚至还当起了向导，指出一些标志性建筑，讲述了当地历史。

到该考虑上大学的事情时，我们毫无疑问都要去上。我们被父母所作出的牺牲鼓舞着，大家都努力地学习以获得学士学位，申请助学金和财政补助。我们也都找了工作，自己挣钱上学。在一家杂货铺打工的过程中，我懂得了一美元所包含的价值。母亲总是提醒我们牢记："工作就是幸福。"

母亲从来不向我们索求什么。有一次，她说："你们不需要为我买什么生日礼物，只要给我写封信，跟我讲讲你们的生活就行了。让我知道你们有没有烦心事，你们过得快不快乐。"

Mama's face was radiant with pride. I knew that everything we had achieved or would achieve was because of my parents.

When we were young children, my mother was, especially, our mentor. Not until I became an adult did I realize how special she was.

Delight in Devotion. My mother was born in a small town in northern Italy. She was three when her parents immigrated to this country in 1926. They lived on Chicago's South Side, where my grandfather worked making ice cream.

Mama thrived in the hectic urban environment. At 16, she graduated first in her high-school class, went on to secretarial school, and finally worked as an executive secretary for a railroad company.

She was beautiful too. When a local photographer used her pictures in his monthly window display, she was flattered. Her favorite portrait showed her sitting by Lake Michigan, her hair windblown, her gaze reaching toward the horizon. My mother always used to say that when you died, God gave you back your "best self ". She'd show us that picture and say, "This is what I'm going to look like in heaven."

My parents were married in 1944. Dad was a quiet and intelligent man who was 17 when he left Italy. Soon after, a hit-and-run accident left him with a permanent limp. Dad worked hard selling candy to Chicago office workers on their break. He had little formal schooling. His English was self-taught. Yet he eventually built a small, successful wholesale candy business. Dad was generous, handsome and deeply religious. Mama was devoted to him.

After she married, my mother quit her job and gave herself to her family.

In 1950, with three children, Dad moved the family to a farm 40 miles from Chicago. He worked the land and commuted to the city to run his business. Mama said goodbye to her parents and friends and traded her busy city neighborhood for a more isolated life. But she never complained. By 1958, our modest white farmhouse was filled with six children, and Mama was delighted.

Think Big. My mother never studied books on parenting. Yet she knew how to raise children. She heightened our self-esteem and helped us reach our potential.

One fall day, I sat at the kitchen table while Mama peeled potatoes. She spied Dad out the window on his tractor and smiled."Your father has accomplished so much." she said proudly, "He really is somebody."

My mother wanted each of us to be somebody too."Your challenge is to be everything you can. Mine is to help." she always said.

She read to us every day and used homemade flash cards to teach us phonetics. She bolstered our confidence, praising even our most ordinary accomplishments. When I was ten, I painted a stack of wooden crates white and nailed them together to make a wobbly bookcase."It's wonderful!" Mama exclaimed."Just what we need." She used it for many years.

In the dining room are two paint-by-number pictures that my sister Gloria and brother Leo did as kids. Several years ago, Leo commented that the pictures weren't very good and offered to take them down. But Mama wouldn't hear of it."They are there to remind you how much you could accomplish even as children." she said.

From the very beginning, she urged us to think big. One day, after visiting our grandparents on the South Side, she made Dad detour past the Prudential Building construction site. Mama explained that when finished, the 41-story building would be Chicago's tallest."Maybe someday one of you can design a building like this." she said.

Her confidence in us was infectious. When my sister Carla was 12, she announced she was going to be a lawyer.

"You can do that." Mama said. "You can do anything you put your mind to."

Tour Guide. To Mama, education was a key part of her blueprint for success. Four of us went to a nearby, one-room school-house. My mother made up for its shortcomings by getting us educational toys, talking to us about history, politics and current events, and helping with home work. The best part of getting a good report card was her unstinting praise.

When I was in the third grade, she urged our teacher to organize a field trip to Chicago museums. My mother helped the teacher rent a bus and plan the trip. She even served as tour guide, pointing out landmarks and recounting local history.

When it came time to think about college, there was never a question that we'd all go. Inspired by our parents'sacrifice, we studied hard to earn scholarships, and applied for grants and financial aid. We also took jobs to earn money for school. Working in a grocery store, I learned the value of a dollar. "Work is a blessing." Mama always reminded us.

She never asked for anything for herself. " You don't have to buy me a birthday present." she said one time, "Instead write me a letter about yourself. " Tell me about your life. Is anything worrying you? Are you happy? "

佚名 / Anonymous

爷爷的藏宝图

客厅里异常安静，钟表的报时声把布里奇特吓了一跳。她转过去，看到桌子上那个雕花的黑色盒子，时钟还在里面咚咚作响，听起来悲哀且空寂。

自爷爷死后，罗斯别墅的一切看起来都是空荡荡的。爷爷在这住了82年，以前每年夏天，布里奇特都要到这来看他。现在这座别墅要卖了。

"你可以留下点儿东西，以纪念爷爷。"妈妈说。

布里奇特不再看着时钟，那不能勾起她对爷爷逗弄的眼睛和拥抱的思念。一本书会让她想起爷爷吗？她走向书架，但大多数的书看起来令人厌烦。这时，她看见一张纸从一本书里露出来，便轻轻地把它搜出来。

纸上一面写着一个日期：1927年2月1日。另一面有些令人激动的东西，布里奇特尖叫一声，她弟弟忙跑了过来。

"看，我发现了什么！"布里奇特说道。

科林接过那张纸，瞥了一眼日期，翻开另一面，顿时说不出话来，在一幅图的上面写着：我的藏宝图。"爷爷总是说他在地里藏了宝物，"布里奇特说，"我以为他在开玩笑呢！""我也是，"科林说，"这张图证明他说的没错。"

这是一张简单的图：一个大圆圈上写着"巨人"，一个箭头从这里指出去，上面写着"步行20码"，箭头的末尾又画了一个小圈，写着"石头"，还有一个叉。

"'巨人'是爷爷叫的那块'大石头'！"布里奇特说。"宝藏就埋在离它20码的小石头下，"科林说，"走，我们去寻宝！"

他们跑出去，从工棚里拿出铁锹，飞一般地穿过田野，跑向那块大石头。爱荷华州农场只有一块大石头，它就在一条小溪边。

科林开始从大石头起步，要用他的小步子量出20码并不容易，但环顾这片原野，能够藏宝的只有两块石头。

　　"先看看这块，"科林边说边挪开较大的那块。

　　布里奇特把她的铲子插入土里，会有什么宝藏呢？"金条，"她想，"还是珠宝——满满一箱蓝宝石和钻石？"

　　这张古老的藏宝图有用吗？

　　科林笑道："现实点儿，布里奇特，我敢打赌，是钱。"

　　"够买一台新计算机或者一辆自行车吗？"

　　"也许足够把这个地方留下，"科林说，"如果我们找到许多钱，妈妈就不用卖掉别墅了。我们就能永远在这过夏天了。"

　　布里奇特知道，这幢别墅没有了爷爷，就和以前大不一样了，但她喜欢这古老的别墅。留下它的愿望激励着她，她握紧铁锹，更用力地挖掘。但是，半个小时过去了，除了挖到泥土，什么都没有。

"一定在另一块石头下面。"科林说。

他们来到另一处，又挖了一个小时，布里奇特的胳膊都酸了，脸也被太阳晒得通红。"这儿也没有宝藏。"她说。她转过身，走回别墅里去。科林咬紧牙，继续挖下去。

布里奇特回到别墅，盯着爷爷的藏宝图。她是不是遗漏了什么东西了呢？有什么线索没有发现呢？她在图片上一英尺一英尺地搜寻，然后翻转过来，唯一的东西就是日期。

"我知道了！"布里奇特叫道。她跑到外面，抓起铁铲，朝着大石头边的小溪跑去。

"你去哪儿？"科林喊道，"等等我。"

科林也冲向小溪，布里奇特已经爬上了那条一直拴在岸边的小船，这是给过河的人准备的。

布里奇特一言不发，他们划过小河。然后，她带路来到了河对岸唯一的一块石头那，没用铁锹，她只是把石头挪到一边，一个金属盒子露了出来。

科林大吃一惊："你怎么知道的？"

布里奇特笑着说："地图是在冬天画的，爷爷从冰上走过来，到了溪对面。"

"我们还忘了一些东西，"她继续说道，"当时是 1927 年，爷爷藏下这个盒子时还是一个小男孩。"

The sound of the clock made Bridget jump. It had been so quiet in the living room. Her eyes went to the carved black case on the desk. Inside it, the clock continued to chime. The notes sounded sad and empty.

Everything seemed empty in Rose Cottage since Grandpa had died. He'd lived here for eighty-two years, and Bridget had visited him every summer of her life. Now the cottage would be sold.

"You can keep something to remember Grandpa by." Mom had said.

Bridget looked away from the clock. That wasn't what she needed to remind her of Grandpa's teasing eyes and his hugs. Would a book make her think of him? She went to the shelf, but most of the books looked boring. Then she saw a paper sticking out of a book. Gently she pulled it out.

A date was written on one side of the paper: February 1st, 1927. On the other side was something exciting. Bridget gave a shout that brought her brother running.

"Look what I found! " Bridget said. Colin took the paper and glanced at the date, then gasped when he saw the other side. Above a drawing were the words "My Treasure Map" . "Grandpa always said he'd buried a treasure on his land, " Bridget said. "I thought he was teasing." "So did I." Colin said. "This map proves that. "

It was a simple map: just a big circle that said The Giant and an arrow pointing from it with the words Twenty-Yard Walk. At the end of the arrow was a small circle marked Stone, and an X.

"The Giant is what Grandpa called that big boulder!" Bridget said. "And the treasure is buried under a stone twenty yards from it, " Colin said, "Let's go! "

They ran outside and grabbed shovels from the shed. They raced across a field to The Giant. It was the only big boulder on the Iowa farm, and it stood beside a stream.

Colin started to walk away from The Giant. It wasn't easy to measure twenty yards with his short strides, but a glance around the field showed only two stones that could hide the treasure.

"This one first," Colin said, rolling aside the bigger stone.

Bridget thrust her shovel into the dirt. What could the treasure be? "Gold bars," she guessed, "Or jewels — a chest full of sapphires and diamonds."

Did the old treasure map make sense? Colin laughed. "Be realistic, Bridget. I'll bet it's money." "Enough to buy a new computer or a bike? " "Maybe enough to save this place, " Colin said. "If we find a lot of money, Mom won't have to sell the cottage. We can always spend our summers here."

Bridget knew it wouldn't be the same without Grandpa, but she loved the old cottage. The thought of saving it spurred her on. She tightened her grip on the shovel and dug harder. But half an hour later, all they'd uncovered was dirt.

"It must be under the other stone." Colin said.

They moved to the other spot and dug for an hour. Bridget's arms began to ache, and her face burned in the sunlight. "The treasure isn't here either." she said. She turned and walked back toward the cottage. Colin gritted his teeth and kept digging.

Bridget went into the cottage and stared at Grandpa's map. Was there something she had missed? Some clue she hadn't snapped up? She searched the drawing inch by inch, then turned over the paper. The only thing there was the date.

"I've got it!" Bridget cried. She raced outside and grabbed her shovel and headed for the stream near The Giant.

"Where are you going?" Colin called. "Wait for me."

Colin dashed to the stream, too. Bridget was already in the rowboat that was always tied near the bank, waiting for anyone who wanted to cross.

Bridget didn't say a word as they rowed across the stream. Then she led the way to a single stone near the opposite bank. She didn't need the shovel. She just rolled aside the stone and uncovered a metal box.

Colin gasped. "How did you know?"

Bridget smiled. "The map was made in the middle of winter. Grandpa crossed the stream. He walked across the ice!"

"There's something else we forgot," she continued, "The year was 1927. Grandpa hid this box when he was a little boy!"

面团 "项链"

The Necklace

英·格洛丽亚·吉文斯
Gloria Givens

我四岁的小儿子凯利上幼儿园了。他每周去幼儿园两次，每次去两个小时。我很快就发现，他总是最后一个离开教室，于是我便去向老师询问情况。"没事，他没遇上什么问题。"老师向我保证道，"他做得挺好的，只是在忙一件很有创意的事情。"

一次，我在教室门口问他是否准备回家了，他大声回答说："不要进来！我要给你一个惊喜。"于是，每天我都会耐心地在外面等他，直到他神神秘秘地笑着出来。

"你在教室里面做些什么啊？"我问他。

"做东西。"他回答说。

我的好奇心愈加强烈。是什么能这么长时间地吸引着他的注意力？他喜欢用字母积木搭建房子，然后接上林肯积木，直到那房屋大得足以停放他的"风火轮"玩具汽车。

这一天终于到来了。他双手捧着他那件具有创意的手工作品，第一个冲出教室。他没有像平

日里那样跑向我，而是一边小心翼翼地朝我的车子走来，一边几乎目不转睛地看着他手中的纸包。他把手中的东西递给我说："妈妈，给你，这是给你的惊喜。我是特地为你做的。"

我小心地掀开纸巾的一边，然后又打开另一边。一串手绘五彩的意大利面团项链就躺在里面。有红色、黄色、绿色、紫色和他的蜡笔盒中其余的每一种颜色。

我谨慎地拿着它转了个方向，阳光透过车窗照在项链上，我夸奖道："太漂亮了，它看上去像一条彩虹项链。"

儿子倚靠在我的胳膊上，和我一起看着项链。他自豪地说："这是我做的，全部是由我一个人做的。"

这串项链给家人带来了一阵欢乐。凯利的爸爸、哥哥和他的两个妹妹都很喜欢它。我小心翼翼地把它放进首饰盒里，以保护它不被弄坏。

晚饭后，我走着去百货商店买牛奶。"等一下，妈妈！"凯利一边在人行道上跑着追我，一边喊着，"您忘记戴项链了。"我弯下腰，他把项链系在我的脖子上。他说："您真好看。"

我脖子上崭新的、颜色明亮的面团项链在商店里引起了人们的轰动。一位陌生人对我说："好漂亮的项链啊。"后来邻居问我："这是你孩子做的？"我点点头作为回答。商店的收银员甚至羡慕地说道："我也想要一条。"

我的衣饰从来没有获得过如此多的赞美，于是，从那儿以后我便经常戴着它，享受人们对它的每一句赞誉。

但是，一段时间过后，项链上的面团珠子一个接一个地碎落了。凯利忘记了这条项链，我也不再戴它，希望上面的珠子可以留存长久一点。有一天，最后一个面团也破碎了，碎屑与首饰盒里的其他面团碎屑混在一起。那条项链不复存在了。我还记得儿子是怎样努力地把它做出

来，而我曾为它感到多么骄傲。想到自己带着
这串项链去做礼拜，参加学校活动，去爷爷家，
我的喉咙便有种哽咽的感觉。这是一份值得纪
念的礼物，我会十分怀念带着它参加的那些各
种家庭活动日。

25 年后的圣诞节前夜，凯利递给我一只小盒子。
"还记得我四岁的时候，很想送您一份礼物，
可是我又没有钱，于是我用线和意大利面团为
您穿成了一条项链，想给您一个惊喜。每次您
把它戴在脖子上，都会让我感觉自己与众不同。
这条项链不结实，所以不能戴得长久。今天，
这份礼物算是对它的弥补吧。"

从红色天鹅绒盒子里面，儿子取出一串美丽的
珍珠项链，并把它戴在我的脖子上。我激动得
快要说不出话来，便打趣地问道："这是你自
己做的吗？"

他咯咯地笑着说："不是。但是我亲手挑选了
每一颗珍珠。我希望这串项链可以给您特别的
感觉，就像以前我送给您的那串那样。圣诞节
快乐，妈妈。"

My younger son, Kelly, started preschool when he was four, attending twice a week for two hours each time. I soon noticed he was always the last one to leave the classroom, so I asked the teacher if he was having problems. "No, no." she assured me, "He is doing fine— just involved in a creative project."

Once I asked through the classroom door if he was ready to leave, he yelled, "Don't come in! It's a surprise." So I waited patiently each day until he finally emerged, smiling and mysterious.

"What are you doing in there? " I asked.

"Making something." he said.

My curiosity was getting the best of me. What held his attention for such a long period of time? He liked building things by stacking alphabet blocks, then attaching Lincoln Logs until he made a structure big enough for parking his Hot Wheel cars.

Eventually the day arrived when he led his class out the door carrying his creative project, with both hands. His eyes rarely left the tissue-wrapped package as he carefully walked to the car, instead of running as usual. He handed it to me. "Here, Mom, it's a surprise. I made it just for you."

Carefully I lifted the tissue off first one side and then the other. Inside nestled a string necklace made of hand-colored macaroni pieces—red, yellow, green, purple and every other color in his crayon box.

"It's beautiful, " I said, holding it carefully and turning it this way and that so the sun shone on it through the car window, "It looks like a rainbow necklace."

He leaned on my arm and stared at it with me. "I made it, " he said confidently, "all by myself."

The necklace caused a lot of excitement at home. Kelly's dad, his older brother and both younger sisters admired it. I carefully stowed it in my jewelry box so it would not get broken.

After dinner I left on a short walk to the grocery store for some milk. "Wait, Mom! Wait!" Kelly yelled as he ran down the sidewalk after me. "You forgot your necklace!" I bent down, and he tied it around my neck. "You look pretty." he said.

My new, brightly colored macaroni necklace caused quite a stir at the market. "Nice necklace." a stranger said. Then my neighbor remarked, "One of your kids make it? " I nodded. The grocery checker even commented, "I want one, too."

Nothing I have ever worn created more comment than that necklace, and I wore it often, enjoying every word.

Over time, however, the macaroni pieces broke one-by-one and slipped off the string. Kelly forgot about the necklace, and I stopped wearing it hoping the pieces would last longer. One day the last piece crumbled and joined the other broken bits of macaroni at the bottom of my jewelry box. The necklace was no more. I remembered how hard he had worked and how proud we had been of his efforts. I got a lump in my throat when I thought about wearing it to church, school events or Grandpa's. It was a memorable gift, and I would miss wearing it for our special family occasions.

Over twenty-five years later, on Christmas Eve, Kelly handed me a small box. "I remember when I was four and wanted to give you a present, but had no money, so I used some string and macaroni to make you a surprise. You were such a good sport about wearing that macaroni necklace, and each time you put it on, you made me feel very special. So this gift is to make up for the macaroni one that didn't last."

He plucked a beautiful string of pearls from inside the red velvet box and placed it around my neck. "Did you make it? " I asked jokingly, barely able to speak.

"No, " he chuckled, "but I did pick out each pearl. I hope this necklace makes you feel as special when you wear it as I felt when you wore the other one. Merry Christmas, Mom."

双重悲伤
Double Sadness

当我们坐在医院的走廊里等待父亲接受检查时，母亲说："我一直为玛莎担心。我们把她留在院子里玩，也没有告诉她我们去哪里。真希望她不会正坐在什么地方哭泣呢。"

我擦干母亲脸颊上挂满的泪水，试图打消她的担心："我就是玛莎，我就陪在您的身边啊。"

"不，你不是。"母亲回答说，"你不是我的小玛莎。"

在尽力去适应父亲突然致残的事实时，过去和现在一直都存在的被抛弃的恐惧笼罩着我们。

前天晚上我们接到电话，父亲摔了一跤，髋部受了伤，并且准备在第二天做更换髋关节的手术。那天晚上，一位朋友陪了母亲一夜。我向母亲许诺说："我会坐早班飞机尽快过去。"

父母结婚有 58 年了。尽管母亲在过去的几个月里头脑越来越糊涂，但是在这之前从来没有发生过什么严重的紧急事情。在我上次回来看望父母的时候，母亲问我："你母亲还健在吗？"那时，她的表情完全是对一位陌生青年女子所表现出的友善的兴趣。而现在，因为日常规律被打乱，父亲也不能一直陪在她的身边，母亲的糊涂状况变得更加严重。

"但是，我为玛莎担心。"当我们回到家，坐下来吃午饭的时候，母亲又一次说起，"我要出去找她。""可是，我就是玛莎啊。"我试着说，"小玛莎长大了，长大成我了。"

"那简直是荒谬。"母亲说道。她用力拉开前门，走上街，紧张地站在那里。她的目光四处搜索着那个她确定早上还见到过的小女孩。可是，什么人也看不到。接着，她又来到房子的后面，穿过后面的空地来到另一条街上。

"我要去问问那边的那些人，看看他们有没有见到我女儿。"母亲变得日益狂乱，几乎会闯入滚滚的车流，穿过繁杂的街道。

我恳求她说："我们回家去吧，给教堂办公室打个电话，没准儿会有谁能帮上忙。"母亲在回家的路上对我说："不跟我说一声就离开，这不大像是玛莎的作风。要么就是她留了字条给我。"

字条！找到缓解母亲情绪的方法了。我们一进到屋里，我就潦草地写了一张字条，并把它放在很容易看到的地方。字条上这样写道："妈妈，我去玛丽·安那里住几天。不要为我担心，我一切都好。玛莎。"

"快看，这里有一张字条。上面都说了些什么？"我说。母亲慢慢地大声读着，很快就平静了下来。

她说："谢天谢地，她一切都好。她和玛丽·安在一起呢。"母亲不安的情绪消除之后，我们坐下来吃完了午饭，并在家里度过了一个平和的下午。

傍晚在医院里的时候，母亲告诉父亲，玛莎去玛丽·安那里住几天，但她还是担心。父亲说："别再另找一个玛莎了，我们有一个玛莎就足够了。"

第二天，玛莎不在身边的事还是让母亲很劳神。她猜测着："她都做些什么事情呢？在没有和我一起事先作好安排之前，她是从来都不会离开的。另外，我希望她能去医院看看爸爸。"

我向母亲保证，说她的女儿很快就会回来。"而且，玛莎是个聪明的小女孩，她能够照顾好自己的。"我说。

"星期天，她需要穿一件干净的裙子去教堂。"母亲说。

"今天才是星期四，时间还多着呢。"我回答。

那晚，在我准备晚饭的时候，母亲问道："你从哪里学会做饭的？你能来这里陪我真好。你有家了吗？"我被母亲接受为一个同伴，而不是女儿，我习惯了与母亲相处的友善方式。

星期五早上，我和母亲去理发、按摩，又去了杂货店。无意间，我听到理发师林恩对母亲说："你女儿能过来陪你，多好啊。"

"她不是我女儿。"母亲低声说，"她的名字和我女儿的一样，但她不是我女儿。"林恩快速地看了我一眼，以便知道是否误解了我们当中谁的意思。而我，只能对她无奈地笑了笑。

在回家的路上，母亲对我说："林恩还以为你是我女儿呢。"

"你不会介意的，是吗？"我问她。

"不会。"她说。

直到哥哥星期六回来，我才又重新被认做家里的一员。那天晚上，母亲说："鲍勃睡在这张床上，你可以在你的老房间里睡。"再次被接纳的感觉真好。

第二天，父亲说："你看，玛莎一直都在这里。根本没必要担心的。"

"但是，这里有一张字条啊！"母亲悲痛地说道。

"那张字条是我写的，"我解释说，"我写它是为了让你在焦虑的时候平静下来。"我看到，有片刻理解的眼神从母亲慢慢昏花的眼中闪过。

"I keep worrying about Martha, " my mother said as we sat in the hospital corridor, waiting for my father to be examined by the doctor. "We left her playing in the yard and didn't tell her where we were going. I hope she's not sitting somewhere crying."

I wiped away tears that were streaming down my cheeks. "But I'm Martha. I'm right here with you." I tried to reassure her.

"No, not you." my mother answered, "My little Martha."

Fears of abandonment, past and present, enveloped us as we tried to adjust to my father's sudden incapacity.

The call had come the night before. My father had fallen and broken his hip; an operation to replace the hip joint was scheduled for the next morning. A friend was staying with my mother for the night." I'll come as soon as I can—on the early morning plane." I promised.

My mother and father, married for fifty-eight years, had never had a serious emergency before, although my mother had become increasingly confused in the last several months. "And is your mother still alive? " she had asked me on my last visit, with a sociable interest in the young woman she had never seen before. Now, with the daily routine disrupted and the nearly constant companionship of my father removed, her disorientation was more severe.

"But I'm worried about Martha." my mother said again when we had returned home and sat down for lunch. "I m going out to look for her." "But I'm Martha." I tried again. "Little Martha grew up and turned into me."

"That's ridiculous." my mother said. She tugged open the front door, went out to the street, and stood tensely. Looking up and down for the little girl she was sure she had seen just that morning. No one in sight. Then to the back of the house and through the back lot to the other street. "I'm going to ask those people over there if they've seen her." My mother, becoming increasingly frantic, was ready to plunge into traffic and cross the busy street.

"Let's go home and call the church office." I pleaded. "Maybe someone there can help." On the way back to the house, my mother said, "It's not like Martha to go away like that without telling me. If only she had left a note."

A note! Seeing a way to relieve my mother's agitation, I scribbled a note as soon as we were in the house, and left it where it could be discovered a minute later. "Mama, " it said, "I have gone to stay with Mary Ann for a few days. Please don't worry. I'm okay. Martha."

"Look, " I said, "here's a note. What does it say? " My mother read it aloud slowly and immediately began to calm down.

"Thank goodness, " she said. "She's all right. She's with Mary Ann." With the tension gone, we sat down to finish lunch and spend a peaceful afternoon at home.

That evening in the hospital, my mother told my father that Martha had gone to stay with Mary Ann for a few days but that she was still worried about her. My father said, "Don't go looking for another Martha. We already have one, and that's enough."

The next day, Martha's absence was still very much on my mother's mind. "What can she be doing? " she wondered. "She's never gone off like that without arranging it with me ahead of time. Besides, I want her to go to the hospital to see Daddy."

I assured my mother that her daughter would come home soon. "Besides, " I said, "Martha is a clever little girl. She can take care of herself."

"She needs a clean dress for church on Sunday. " my mother said.

"It's only Thursday, " I replied, "Plenty of time."

"Where did you learn to take over a kitchen like this? " my mother asked as I fixed dinner that night."It's nice of you to come and stay with me. Do you have a family? " Having been accepted as a companion, if not a daughter, I settled into an amicable routine with my mother.

Friday morning we went to the hairdresser, the chiropractor, and the grocery store. I overheard Lynne, the hairdresser, say to my mother, "It's nice that your daughter could come to stay with you."

"That's not my daughter." my mother confided, "she has the same name, but she's not my daughter." Lynne looked quickly at me to see if she had misunderstood one of us, and I gave her a rueful smile.

On the way home my mother said, "Lynne thought you were my daughter."

"You don't mind, do you? " I asked.

"No." she said.

It wasn't until my brother came on Saturday that I was recognized as part of the family. "Bob will take this bed, and you can sleep in your old room." my mother said that night. It felt good to be legitimate again.

"You see," my father said the next day, "Martha has been here all the time.

There was no need to worry."

"But there was a note!" my mother wailed.

"I wrote the note," I explained, "I wrote it to calm you when you were so anxious. " And comprehension flickered for a moment in my mother's gradually dimming eyes.

[英]玛丽·马尔丹特 / Mary Marcdante

Squeeze My Hand and I'll Tell You that I Love You

递给母亲的
甜蜜抚慰

小时候跌倒了受伤后的情形，你还记得吗？还记得妈妈是怎样抚慰我们的伤痛的吗？在这种情形下，我的妈妈雷格斯·罗斯就会把我抱起，放到她的床上，亲吻我摔痛的地方。然后，坐在我身旁，握住我的小手说："痛的时候，握紧我的手，我会告诉你我爱你。"一次又一次，我握紧了她的手。无一例外的是，每次我都能听到她说："玛丽，我爱你。"

我发现，有时自己会假装受伤，那样做只是为了得到她这样的抚慰。尽管这种抚慰的形式伴随着我的成长而有所变化，但是她总会找出一种方法抚慰我的伤痛，增加我生命中各个角落的欢乐。高中生活中的那些艰难的日子里，妈妈会在我回家的时候给我准备好她最喜欢的"荷西"巧克力。20岁的时候，妈妈时常会打电话给我，提议去易斯特布鲁克公园野餐，庆祝威斯康星州温暖明媚的日子。妈妈和爸爸来我家探望过我之后，便会有一张手写的感谢便条邮寄过来，那是为了提醒我：对她来说，我这个女儿是多么重要。

然而，最令我记忆深刻的抚慰，还是小时候妈妈握着我的手说："痛的时候，握紧我的手，我会告诉你我爱你。"

我30多岁的一天早晨，爸爸在我上班的时候打来电话。爸爸做事一向有条不紊，但那天我从他的声音中听出了慌乱不安。要知道，前天晚上妈妈和爸爸刚来看望过我。爸爸说："玛丽，你妈妈出了点儿问题，可是我不知道该怎么办。你尽快回来吧。"

开车到父母家的10分钟车程中，恐惧充斥着我的头脑。一路上，我都在猜测着妈妈出了什么事。到家的时候，我看到父亲正在厨房里忙，而妈妈则躺在床上。她闭着双眼，双手放在胃上。我用尽可能平静的声音轻唤她："妈妈，我在你身边呢。"

"是玛丽吗？"

"是的。妈妈。"

"玛丽，真的是你吗？"

"是的，妈妈。真的是我。"

我没想到母亲会问下一个问题，当我听到这个问题时，我不寒而栗，无言以对。

"玛丽，我是不是要死了？"

看到亲爱的妈妈如此无助地躺在那里，我的泪水在心里开了闸。

我的思绪很乱，直到脑子里闪出这样一个问题："如果是我这样问，妈妈会如何回答？"

一时间我无言以对，这一刻似乎停滞了百万年。"妈妈，我不知道您是否会死，但是如果您愿意，一切都会平安的。我爱你。"

妈妈哭了，她说："玛丽，我痛得很厉害。"

该说些什么呢？我又一次迟疑了。坐在母亲床前，握住她的手，我听见了自己的声音："妈妈，疼的话，就握紧我的手，我爱你，妈妈。"

她紧紧抓住了我的手。

"妈妈，我爱你。"

在接下来的两年里，直到她因卵巢癌去世，我和妈妈有过无数次握手，传递过无数声"我爱你"。我们无法知道我们的关键时刻何时会出现，但此刻我知道，当它真正到来时，无论我是和谁在一起，我都会时刻传递妈妈的甜蜜抚慰："痛的时候，握紧我的手，我会告诉你我爱你。"

Remember when you were a child and you fell and hurt yourself? Do you remember what your mother did to ease the pain? My mother, Grace Rose, would pick me up, carry me to her bed, sit me down and kiss my "owwie". Then she'd sit on the bed beside me, take my hand in hers and say, "When it hurts, squeeze my hand and I'll tell you that I love you." Over and over I'd squeeze her hand, and each time, without fail, I heard the words, "Mary, I love you."

Sometimes, I'd find myself pretending I'd been hurt just to have that ritual with her. As I grew up, the ritual changed, but she always found a way to ease the pain and increase the joy I felt in any area of my life. On difficult days during high school, she'd offer her favorite Hershey chocolate almond bar when I returned home. During my 20s, Mom often called to suggest a spontaneous picnic lunch at Estabrook Park just to celebrate a warm, sunny day in Wisconsin. A handwritten thank-you note arrived in the mail after every single visit she and my father made to my home, reminding me of how special I was to her.

But the most memorable ritual remained her holding my hand when I was a child and saying, "When it hurts, squeeze my hand and I'll tell you that I love you."

One morning, when I was in my late 30s, following a visit by my parents the night before, my father phoned me at work. He was always commanding and clear in his directions, but I heard confusion and panic in his voice. "Mary, something's wrong with your mother and I don't know what to do. Please come over as quickly as you can."

The 10-minute drive to my parents' home filled me with dread, wondering what was happening to my mother. When I arrived, I found Dad pacing in the kitchen and Mom lying on their bed. Her eyes were closed and her hands rested on her stomach. I called to her, trying to keep my voice as calm as possible. "Mom, I'm here."

"Mary?"

"Yes, Mom."

"Mary, is that you?"

"Yes, Mom, it's me."

I wasn't prepared for the next question, and when I heard it, I froze, not knowing what to say.

"Mary, am I going to die?"

Tears welled up inside me as I looked at my loving mother lying there so helpless.

My thoughts raced, until this question crossed my mind: What would Mom say?

I paused for a moment that seemed like a million years, waiting for the words to come. "Mom, I don't know if you're going to die, but if you need to, it's okay. I love you."

She cried out, "Mary, I hurt so much."

Again, I wondered what to say. I sat down beside her on the bed, picked up her hand and heard myself say, "Mom, when it hurts, squeeze my hand and I'll tell you that I love you."

She squeezed my hand.

"Mom, I love you."

Many hand squeezes and "I love you's" passed between my mother and me during the next two years, until she passed away from ovarian cancer. We never know when our moments of truth will come, but I do know now that when they do, whomever I'm with, I will offer my mother's sweet ritual of love every time. "When it hurts, squeeze my hand and I'll tell you that I love you."

命中注定的艳情
An Unlikely Hero

[美] 托尼·卢 / Tony Lu

当古尔利克森博士正在为实验心理学课安排研究小组时，我默默地祈祷他能够把我与一个可爱的女生，至少是一个志趣相投的同学分在一组。总而言之，我希望他不要让我与那个具有强烈竞争意识、异常严肃的家伙做搭档，这个人总爱穿着深颜色的衣服，并且个性十足。经过一番深思熟虑之后，古尔利克森博士公布了分组决定，宣布我与一个我最想躲避的人成为一组，这就像命中注定似的。

我走到自己的实验搭档面前，作了自我介绍。他看着我的样子，仿佛我并不存在似的。我感觉到，他似乎认为我会阻碍他进步，并且很可能导致他的平均成绩直线下降。他并不完全怀有恶意，只是给了我这样的印象，无论什么实验，如果他独自去做就会做得更好。我的加入似乎只会妨碍他的研究，只能成为他不得不花时间和精力应付的麻烦，因为他是一个能够独立完成任务的人，他有重要的事情要做。

当然，我不想把整个学期都荒废掉，为了不让事情变得更加糟糕，我什么也没说，只是尽力把实验做好。

根据计划，每个实验小组要提出假设，作实验检验假设，作统计学分析，介绍研究结果。小组所取得的成绩就是每个小组成员的成绩。我每次都忐忑不安地与同伴讨论实验的问题，他的专注和优秀的成绩是出了名的，他是一个勇于挑战的人。正相反，我与他相差甚远，事实上，我心里曾经闪现过逃课的念头。然而，我不想被他看扁，所以很快放弃了这种想法。我向那些忙于工作的朋友请教我该如何去做，他们的答复全部是：无论发生什么，你都要坚持到最后。

经过长时间的讨论之后，我们终于达成一致，决定作一项关于空间触觉和动觉感知的研究。我们已经确定了题目，虽然我并不明白这是一项什么研究。为了制订计划，我们定期碰面，每次讨论决定之后，我都觉得制订计划的是他，而不是我。我们碰面的次数越多，我对他的才智和直击问题核心的能力就越憎恨。我逐渐意识到，他的水平比我高很多。他很了解技术方面的知识，并且能够带着非常明确的目标去处理细节问题。

另一方面，我能提出的建议微乎其微，看起来似乎很幼稚。有一次，我鼓起勇气问他，他为什么那么紧张严肃。他回答说，他没有闲聊的时间，对他来说，无聊的人和事情只是浪费时间，这让我感到惊讶。他甚至告诉我，许多所谓的朋友只会让人分心，因此，他没有结交很多朋友。不过，他补充说，一旦选择某人作为自己的朋友，他就会把他们当做一生的朋友。他的冷淡和愤世嫉俗让我感到非常震惊，当时，我恨不得这个学期马上结束。

一学期的时光慢慢过去，我们尝试设计了一个非常出色的实验，而且实验操作也很简单。挑选志愿做实验对象的学生成为我们工作的一部分，我决定致力于招募研究对象，而他负责阐述科学方法。我抓住一切可能的机会作贡献，然而，我仍然有一种感觉：他才是整个实验的推动力量。

有一天，我得知他生病住进了医院。很显然，他是因为溃疡出血才住进医院的。他想取得最好的成绩，想找一份工作，想帮助生病的女朋友度过危险期，他背负的这些压力把他压垮了。

当去医院看望这个坚忍克己的实验伙伴时，我第一次发现，他的脸上有了一种脆弱的表情。我知道，他是担心我会把实验搞砸，担心他非常高的平均成绩被小组实验成绩给毁掉，甚至会突然失掉进研究院的机会。我告诉他，应该一心一意恢复健康，并保证我一定会付出最大的努力，不会让他失望的。我们都很清楚，我必须比最好做得还要好。

任务非常艰巨，我埋头整理统计资料，这些资料已经超出了我的理解范围。我对有生以来所做的任何作业，都不曾付出这么多的时间和精力。我不能让他看到我失败，不愿意因为我而影响他的成绩。为了能够利用一切安静的时间作研究，我把工作时间调整到夜里，从午夜一直干到早晨六点，工作耗费了我许多时间。我感觉自己全身心地投入到一场挑战中，但现在的问题是，我能胜任吗？

在本学期即将结束的时候，各个小组终于要在所有组合小组前陈述自己的研究成果了。轮到我们组的时候，我使用自己的表演技巧阐述了他的科学方法，我竭尽了全力。我们得了"A"，这让我感到异常惊喜！

当我告诉实验伙伴，我们共同的努力取得了成功时，他笑着感谢我完成了实验。那一刻，某些东西将我们联系在一起，这些特别的东西，与信赖有关，与分享获奖的喜悦有关。

这些年来，我们仍然保持着密切的联系。通过不断的学习，他获得了博士学位，并与大学女友建立了家庭。

那个学期，我学到的不仅仅是统计学分析和实验过程。他是我生活中的另类英雄，我的生活因他而面临挑战，因他而变得广阔。

事实证明，他是正确的，我们成了终身的朋友。

When Dr. Gullickson was assigning project mates for his introduction to experimental psychology class, I secretly hoped he would pair me with a cute coed or at least a classmate I could have some fun with. Above all, I hoped he wouldn' t assign me to work with the intense, fiercely competitive, singularly serious fellow who always wore dark clothes and apparently had a personality to match. As fate would have it, Dr. Gullickson very deliberately matched everyone in class and announced that I would be working with the one person in class I wanted to avoid.

I went up to my new lab mate and introduced myself. He looked at me as though I weren't there. I felt he treated me as though I would hold him back and probably cause his grade-point average to take a nosedive. He wasn't outright mean or abusive. He just gave me the impression he could do whatever project we dreamed up better if he did it alone. He was a loner, and I could only impede his research. He had important things to do, and I was going to be something of an annoyance he' d have to deal with.

Needless to say, I didn't look forward to an entire semester of being brushed off,but I tried to make the best of it and didn' t say anything, lest I make things worse.

The project required each lab team to develop a hypothesis, set up an experiment to test the hypothesis, run the tests, do the statistical analysis and present the findings. Whatever grade the team received would be shared by both students. When my lab mate and I met to discuss our project, I was uneasy. Here was this challenging student who had a reputation for single-mindedness and good grades—the exact opposite of me. I was outmatched. I actually wanted to drop the class at one point, but stopped short because I didn't want to give him the satisfaction of my chickening out. I asked my friends at work what I should do, and the overall response was to stick it out no matter what.

After lengthy discussions, we somehow agreed to do a study on the tactile-kinesthetic perception of space. I wasn't sure what it meant, but at least we had a topic. We started to meet regularly to formulate our plans, and every time I felt the project was more his than mine. The more we met, the more I resented his intelligence and his ability to cut through to the core issues. And I was aware he was much more advanced than me. He knew technical things and approached every detail with great singularity of purpose.

I, on the other hand, must have seemed naive, with little to offer. At one point I summoned up my courage and asked him why he seemed so uptight and serious. To my surprise, he replied that he didn't have time for small talk or petty people and things that would waste his time. He even went on to say that he didn't have many friends because most so-called friends were just a distraction. But, he added, when he did choose someone to be his friend, they would be a friend for life. I was floored by his cold and cynical response. Right then and there, I realized the end of the semester couldn't come soon enough.

As the semester wore on, we tried to fashion a simple yet elegant experiment. Part of our job was to select students who had volunteered to be subjects for our project. I decided to devote myself to the task of working with the subjects, while he developed the scientific model. I put in my two cents'worth whenever I could, but I still felt he was the driving force.

Then one day I got word that he was in the hospital. Apparently, he had been admitted for a hemorrhaging ulcer. The stress of getting the best grades, holding down a job and helping his girlfriend through the medical crisis she was going through had taken its toll on him.

When I visited him in the hospital, I noticed for the first time a sense of vulnerability on the face of my stoic lab mate. I knew that he was aware that I could blow the experiment, and our shared grade would shatter his lofty G. P. A. and possibly derail his chances for graduate school. I assured him I would not let him down and he should only concentrate on getting better. I would do my best. We both knew I'd have to do better than my best.

I had a formidable task ahead of me. I was in over my head, running the statistical data. I poured more time and energy into that project than I had ever done on any assignment in my life. I was not going to let him see me fail and have it reflect on him. I was working the graveyard shift at my job, so I used whatever quiet time from midnight to 6:00 A. M. to work on the project. The work consumed me. There was a sense of challenge that completely overtook me. The question remained: Was I up to it?

Eventually, the semester came to a close, and each team had to present its findings in front of the assembled class. When it was our turn, I did my level best to present his scientific methodology with my showmanship. To my amazement, we were awarded an A!

When I told my lab mate about our shared triumph, he smiled and thanked me for carrying on. Something connected then. Something special. It had to do with trust and the exhilaration of sharing a common prize.

We have stayed close throughout the years. He went on to achieve a doctorate. He also went on to marry his college girlfriend.

I learned more than statistical analysis and experimental procedures that semester. My life has been enhanced by our encounter and challenged by this man, who became my unlikely hero.

And in the end, he was right: we have become friends for life.

非同一般的友谊

Friends for Life

[美] 蒂娜·利兹 / Tina Leeds

蒂姆周六出发去大学报到，我周日出发。从上高中以来，这是我们第一次分离。我们之间的亲密关系让别人很是羡慕，尽管这种友谊超越了一般的男女朋友。我崇拜他与众不同的个性、他让人觉得可笑的笑话和他孩子气的长相。他很了解我，能够说出我没有说完的话，他的一个眼神，就可以让我开怀大笑。我们

FRIENDS FOR LIFE

爱慕着彼此，在高中最后一个暑假来临的时候，我们之间的友情变得更加深厚了。

夏季缓缓地来临了，蒂姆正在努力让我忘记那个性情古怪的人，与他在一起完全是浪费时间，现在，我称呼这个人为前男友。几个月以来，蒂姆一直与我的一个好朋友约会。她常常挖苦他，在朋友们面前捉弄他，最后与他分手，让他哭泣，然而我只能坐在一旁看着。她伤了我最好的朋友的心，这就和伤了我的心一样。

我们打电话互相倾诉至深夜，彼此安慰，互相出主意，一起为上大学的事情担心。在那个夏天接下来的日子里，我们共度了所有的时光，那时我们两个人都是单身。在深夜结束一天的工作之后，我们就约在咖啡馆见面，一待就是几个小时，只是坐在那里聊天。那个夏天，我们之间的友情变得更加深厚。至今，我仍然无法了解，为什么在两个人准备上大学时，我们的友情竟然变得如此亲密。

去新学校报到的日子越来越近，我们不得不向彼此告别了。我们一起去购买上学用的物品，并且计划着上大学一个月之后聚会。

那个星期六的早晨，我愁肠百结，怀着紧张不安的心情开车送他去学校。在三个小时的路程中，我一直想搞清楚自己是怎么了。我当然会思念他，然而那是一种紧张的心情，而不是悲伤。我们把行李搬进了那个很小的房间，并把房间整理得像家一样。这时，我终于明白了自己的感情，深刻地体会到那是一种什么样的感情。我爱上了眼前的这个家伙！这是一种更加深厚的感情，不是高中时的那种友谊之爱，这让我感到无助。我终于了解了自己对最好朋友

FRIE
FOR
LIFE

174

NDS

的真实感情，这似乎太迟了。我坐在他的床上，泪水溢满了眼眶。我向自己最要好的朋友，也是我所爱的人道别，心中不停地想，我们能否真的像约定的那样，一个月后见到彼此呢？

那天晚上在家收拾行李的时候，一想到可能发生变化的未来，我恐惧地哭了。我们都会有各自的生活，也许很少会想起对方。就在那个时候，电话响了，我把眼泪擦掉，努力用平静的语调问好，电话那头传出的声音让我知道一切都进行得很顺利——是蒂姆。我甚至还没有来得及问好，蒂姆就急切地对我说："蒂娜，我们能不能早点儿见面，今晚可以吗？"

FRIENDS FOR LIFE

我还没有完全挂上电话，就情不自禁地咧开嘴笑了起来。我跳上车子，向他的学校驶去。我是如何在那么短的时间内赶到学校的（我用了 1 小时 45 分钟），这已经无关紧要了，重要的是见到他的那一刻，我拥抱了他，告诉他我爱他。事实上，我曾经那样做过无数次。然而，他这次把我从怀里推开，注视着我的眼睛说，他爱我，然后吻了我。这个吻似乎包含着几个月，甚至几年来彼此付出的真情。

第二天早晨出发前往学校的时候，我的整个脑袋、整颗心想的全是蒂姆。当我拿出钱包掏钱买汽水时，一张小纸条掉了出来。那是蒂姆写给我的，直到现在，我一想起上面的话语仍然会开心地微笑："蒂娜，我对自己感到很气愤，为什么这么晚才向你表白……我爱你!"感动的泪水夺眶而出，我感到了真正的幸福，对我们的关系也安下心来。

我依然保留着蒂姆写给我的纸条，我们一直保持着那种非同一般的友谊，直到永远。只是，现在我们分享了更多的东西——三个漂亮的孩子和同一个姓氏。

Tim left for college on a Saturday and I on a Sunday. It would be the first time we had ever been apart over the course of our high school friendship. Ours was more than a normal boy/girl friendship, though. Our close connection was the envy of others. I was in awe of his amazing personality, his hilarious jokes and his little-boy looks. He could read my mind, finish my sentences and bring me to hysterical laughter with only a look.

We adored each other. As our last summer together approached, our bond only grew.

The summer started off slowly, with Tim trying to get my mind off the jerk I now refer to as my ex-boyfriend and a total waste of my time. Tim was dating one of my close friends, and had been for a couple of months. I had to sit by and watch as she ridiculed him, made a joke of him in front of our friends, and eventually made him cry when she finally ended it. She broke my best friend's heart, and I ached with him.

We spent hours talking on the phone late at night, comforting each other, giving each other advice and worrying about college. Over the rest of the summer, both of us were single, so we spent all of our time together. Late at night after work, we would meet at cafes and just talk for hours. We grew even closer that summer. I only wondered why our friendship had to get so close now, as we were both preparing to leave for college.

As the time approached when we would have to say good-bye, we went shopping together for school supplies and planned our first rendezvous as college students for a month after we were both at school.

As I left that Saturday morning to take him to school, I was extremely nervous, my stomach full of knots. I kept wondering what was wrong with me during the three-hour car ride. Of course I was going to miss him, but this was not a sad feeling, this was nervousness. As we finished packing him into his tiny room and making it feel like some semblance of home, it hit me—and it hit me hard. I was in love with this guy! And it wasn't the friendship kind of love that I had felt for him throughout high school; it was something much deeper. I felt helpless. I had finally realized my true feelings for my best friend when it was too late. Tears filled my eyes as I sat on his springy, steel bed. I said good-bye to my best friend and the love of my life, wondering if we were really going to meet in a month as planned.

That night at home as I packed my stuff I cried, scared that things would never be the same. We were both going to have our separate lives and would probably barely think of each other. Just then the phone rang, and as I wiped my tears and tried to utter a quiet hello, the voice on the other end let me know everything was going to be okay. It was Tim. Before even saying hello he blurted out, "Tina, we're going to make that rendezvous earlier than I thought. How about tonight?"

I was grinning like crazy as I practically hung up on him, jumped in my car without directions and headed for his school. How I got there in such a short time (an hour and forty-five minutes) is irrelevant. What is relevant is that the second I got there, I hugged him and told him I loved him. I had actually done that numerous times before, but this time he pulled away from my embrace, looked into my eyes, told me he loved me, too—and then kissed me. It was a kiss that seemed to contain months, even years, worth of love for each other.

When I left for school the next morning, I had Tim on my mind and in my heart. As I picked up my wallet to get money out to pay for a soda, a tiny piece of paper fell out. It was from Tim and contained words that touch my heart to this day and still make me smile. "Tina, I am so mad at myself for waiting to tell you... I love you!" My eyes welled up with tears, and I felt truly happy and at ease with our situation.

I still keep that note from Tim, and we continue to share a remarkable friendship and always will. Only these days we also share much more—three beautiful children and the same last name.

让我做你的声音

佚名 / Anonymous

A SILENT LOVE

最初，女孩的家里人强烈反对她和这个男孩约会。理由是家境不般配，要是和他一起生活，女孩将来会吃很多苦。

因为家庭的压力，两人常常吵架。尽管女孩深爱着男孩，可她总是问："你爱我有多深？"

男孩不太会说话，常常令女孩伤心。因为这个原因，再加上家庭的压力，

女孩常常对男孩发脾气。而他，只是用沉默接受这一切。

过了几年，男孩终于毕业了，他打算到国外去深造。临走之前，他向女孩求婚："我不善于表达，然而我知道我爱你。假如你接受我，我愿意用我的余生来照顾你。至于你的家人，我会尽力说服他们接受我。你愿意嫁给我吗？"

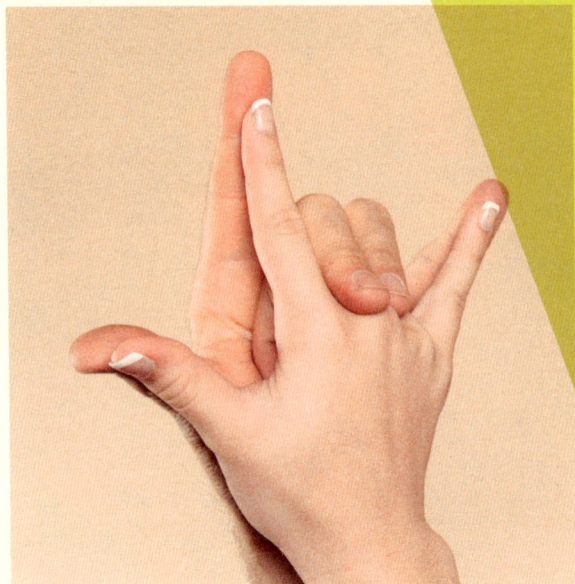

女孩答应了，男孩凭借他的决心得到了女孩家里人的同意，他们可以结婚了。因此，在他离开前，他们订了婚。

女孩进入社会工作，而男孩则在国外继续他的学业。他们通过电子邮件和电话传递爱意，虽然这样很辛苦，然而他们从未想过放弃。

有一天，女孩在上班途中被一辆失控的汽车撞倒了。醒来之后，女孩看到父母都坐在床边，她意识到自己伤得厉害。看到妈妈在哭，她想安慰她，然而她意识到从她嘴里发出的只是一声叹息，她失声了……

医生解释说，是因为大脑的损伤使她不能出声。听着父母的安慰，她却说不出一个字，她伤心欲绝。

在医院的那段日子，陪伴她的除了无声的哭泣，还是无声的哭泣。出院之后，所有的事情还是老样子，除了电话铃声。每当电话一响，这个声音就会刺穿她的心。她不想让他知道这一切，不想让自己成为他的负担，因此她写了一封信，告诉他，她不想再等下去了。

她把订婚戒指连同那封信一块儿寄给了他，男孩写了无数封回信，打了无数个电话。而女孩所能做的，除了痛哭，还是痛哭……

她的父母决定搬家，想让她忘掉这一切，重新快乐起来。

在新环境下，女孩学会了手语，开始了崭新的生活，她每天都告诉自己必须忘记他。有一天，一个朋友到她的家里来，告诉她，他已经回来了，她请朋友不要把所发生的一切告诉他。从此以后，她再也没有听到他的任何消息。

一年过去了，朋友带给她一个信封，信封里是男孩的结婚喜帖。女孩的心都碎了，然而在她打开之后，看到的是自己的名字。

就在她要问朋友怎么回事的时候，她看到男孩出现在她的面前。他用手语告诉她："我花了一年的时间来学习手语，我只是想让你知道，我没有忘记我们的诺言。让我做你的声音吧，我爱你。"说着，他将戒指重新戴到她的手上。终于，女孩露出了笑脸。

From the very beginning, the girl's family objected strongly on her dating this guy, saying that it had got to do with family background and that the girl would have to suffer for the rest of her life if she were to be with him.

Due to family's pressure, the couple quavered very often. Though the girl loved the guy deeply, she always asked him, "How deep is your love for me?"

As the guy was not good with his words, this often caused the girl to be very upset. With that and the family's pressure, the girl often vented her anger on him. As for him, he only endured it in silence.

After a couple of years, the guy finally graduated and decided to further his studies overseas. Before leaving, he proposed to the girl. "I'm not very good with words. But all I know is that I love you. If you allow me, I will take care of you for the rest of my life. As for your family, I'll try my best to talk them round. Will you marry me?"

The girl agreed, and with the guy's determination, the family finally gave in and agreed to let them get married. So before he left, they got engaged.

The girl went out to the working society, whereas the guy was overseas, continuing his studies. They sent their love through emails and phone calls. Though it was hard, both never thought of giving up.

One day, while the girl was on her way to work, she was knocked down by a car that lost control. When she woke up, she saw her parents beside her bed. She realized that she was badly injured. Seeing her mum crying, she wanted to comfort her. But she realized that all that could come out of her mouth was just a sigh. She lost her voice...

The doctors said that the impact on her brain had caused her to lose her voice. Listening to her parents' comfort, but with nothing coming out from her, she broke down.

During the stay in hospital, besides silent cry... it was still just silent cry that accompanied her. Upon reaching home, everything seemed to be the same, except for the ringing tone of the phone, which pierced into her heart every time it rang. She did not wish to let the guy know, and not want to be a burden to him. She wrote a letter to him saying that she did not wish to wait any longer.

With that, she sent the ring back to him. In return, the guy sent millions and millions of reply, and countless of phone calls... All the girl could do, besides crying, was still crying...

The parents decided to move away, hoping that she could eventually forget everything and become happy.

With a new environment, the girl learned sign language, and started a new life, telling herself every day that she must forget the guy. One day, her friend came and told her that he's back. She asked her friend not to let him know what happened to her. Since then, there wasn't any more news of him.

A year had passed and her friend came with an envelope containing an invitation card for the guy's wedding. The girlwas shattered. When she opened the letter she saw her name in it instead.

When she was about to ask her friend what's going on, she saw the guy standing in front of her. He used sign language telling her "I've spent a year's time to learn sign language. Just to let you know that I've not forgotten our promise.

Let me have the chance to be your voice. I love you."With that, he slipped the ring back into her finger. The girl finally smiled.